MW01005969

Front Cover: Norrod's Hemphill Maud.
Back Cover: Sequan Mike.

Frontispiece: Hudson's Tex

Front Endpapers: Sequan Grizzly
Back Endpapers: Isaacs' Princess and her
son Jake working the springpole

ISBN 0-87666-734-5

© Copyright 1981 by T.F.H. Publications
Inc., Ltd.

Distributed in the U.S. by T.F.H. Publications, Inc., 211 West Sylvania
Avenue, PO Box 427, Neptune, NJ 07753; in England by T.F.H. (Gt. Britain)
Ltd., 13 Nutley Lane, Reigate, Surrey; in Canada to the pet trade by Rolf C.
Hagen Ltd., 3225 Sartelon Street, Montreal 382, Quebec; in Southeast Asia
by Y.W. Ong, 9 Lorong 36 Geylang, Singapore 14; in Australia and the South
Pacific by Pet Imports Pty. Ltd., P.O. Box 149, Brookvale 2100, N.S.W.
Australia; in South Africa by Valid Agencies, P.O. Box 51901, Randburg 2125
South Africa. Published by T.F.H. Publications, Inc., Ltd, the British Crown
Colony of Hong Kong.

The Book of

The American
Pit Bull Terrier

Richard F. Stratton

Powell's Boots, a two-time winner and a son of Burton's Hank, descendant of Jimmy Boots.

Opposite:
Hammonds' Queenie, black and tan, from Willie and Elliston's Duchess. Pure Hammonds breeding.

Contents

tion" to You Too . . . Bulldog Triumphs . . . Vendetta
. . . The Chicken Cure . . . Liza on the Ice

Getting on the Stick . . . Spanky and Hutch . . . Cruiser
Mistaken for Milkbone . . . The B Factor . . . Tough
Test for Coons

Formal letter against legislation making dog fighting a
felony

Law: Penal Code 597.5 Dog Fights—Training, Conducting, Attending

Catch 'Em & Fetch 'Em . . . Schutzhund Dog (protection dog) . . . Pit Bulls Are Where You Find Them

"PR" Red Rosie.

Opposite:
Casey Jones' dog Hutch.

Acknowledgments

So many people have helped me in so many ways that it is difficult, if not impossible, to properly thank them all. I would, however, like to express appreciation in particular to Jack Kelly, the editor of *Sporting Dog Journal* for providing me with many of the photographs contained herein and to the American Dog Breeder's Association (who publish *Pit Bull Gazette*) for providing me with pictures from their files. I also feel a need to proclaim gratitude for the help provided me by the late Colonel Wilbur Barnes, perhaps one of the foremost authorities on the colored Bull Terrier while he was alive. He was not in agreement with me on many subjects, but I enjoyed the polemics of our discussions, and he was gracious enough to permit me the use of his very fine library (which contained original copies of Stonehenge and Idestone) even though he must have known I would use it to shore up my "heresies"!

My thanks go also to my good friend, Kent Freeman, without whose photographic talents this book could never have been so well illustrated. Most of the best color photos in it were taken by Mr. Freeman, including the front cover picture of a great family dog, Riptide Belle.

Dedication

This book is dedicated with warmth and affection to my father- and mother-in-law, Sam and Stella Slosky, and to their daughter, Stephanie, who had the good sense to marry well!

"PR" Apache Pancho Villa (age 7 months). Sire: Apache Red Baron.
Dam: Apache Gypsy.

Opposite above:
Dickie Freeman with Burton's
Dillinger, an extremely game
dog, grandson of Hondo and of
the famous Eli.

Opposite:
Gehres' Bravo, of Sorrell's
breeding.

Foreword

This book is intended as an advanced work of sorts for those who already know something about the American Pit Bull Terrier. In fact, the presumption is so strong that the reader has already at least perused my other book *(This Is The American Pit Bull Terrier)* that I have not bothered to define terms or to explain elementary things. All this was done in the first book. If, however, you do not have the other book, please do not feel you must drop this one until you've read the other. Relax. (You can get the other one later!) You may be confused by a few things, but hopefully they will eventually become clear as you get into the book.

One of the primary sources of confusion will be the number of different names that are bandied about. While the formal name for our breed is the American Pit Bull Terrier, he is more commonly called "Bulldog" in casual conversation or even in writings done for other Pit Bull people. Oh, yes, "Pit Bull" is another nickname for the breed, as is "Pit Bull Terrier", "Pit Bulldog", and "Pit Terrier", to name just a few additional ones! (I once advocated not capitalizing nicknames for the breed, but most people, myself included, found that overly confusing. Anyway, news journalists don't capitalize breed names at all. But then you run into silly problems such as "American pit bull terrier" and "Chesapeake Bay retriever"!)

To compound the confusion, there are other breeds that are occasionally confused with ours, namely the Bulldog (the pushed-in nose type), the Bull Terrier (white and colored), the Staffordshire Bull Terrier and most of all, the American Staffordshire Terrier. Actually, the only breed our dogs are at all close to is the American Staffordshire Terrier, as they were the same breed nearly fifty years ago. Some people claim they are still the same breed, but those people are distinctly in the minority. While we're at it, the American Staffordshire Terrier has a nickname too. It is referred to as the "Staff" (or "Staf") or the "Am Staff" (or "Am Staf"). The Staffordshire Bull Terrier is called the "Stafford."

Since the Bulldog fraternity extends back into antiquity, it has a vocabulary of its own. Most of the terminology can be deciphered by contextual clues. However, some terms mean different things within the Pit Bull culture than they do in the rest of the world. A "cur", for example, can be a pure-bred dog. Confused? Well, you may end up having to get the other book after all. If you end up with the Pit Bull "fever" (as you most likely will), you won't even mind.

Richard F. Stratton

Sequan Invictus, son of Going Light Barney out of Feather, a deservedly famous bitch by Stu Fowler out of Going Light Penny, Barney's mother.

"PR" Apache Abbey Normal (age 18 months). Sire: Wise's Max-imillian. Dam: Apache Red Lady.

Greenwood's Granny (previously known as Hansons's Ginger Snap). This bitch was a full sister to one of the greatest of all modern brood bitches, Carver's Black Widow.

Chapter 1

A Sheep In Wolf's Clothing

One of the pitfalls to communication lies in that little phrase "It's obvious!" What is obvious to A, alas, is by no means obvious to B and is downright ludicrous to C.

Isaac Asimov

In 1976 my book *This Is The American Pit Bull Terrier* was published. While to me it seemed an innocuous little book on a much-maligned breed, it had the impact of an artillery shell on the dog world generally. While many hailed the book as a breath of fresh air, groups were formed with the express purpose of debunking it. Among a large group of people I was automatically branded a dog fighter. The book was quoted in a number of Sunday supplement articles on either dog fighting generally or the breed specifically. I was ready to debate in print anyone who wanted to challenge any of the premises of the book, but there were few challenges. Most critical comment was placed furtively in private club bulletins, *and I was not sent copies.* Oh, well, at least the book was noticed!

Since I plan to go into even more detail about dogfighting than I did in the previous book, it might be in order for me to tell something about myself and my attitudes on a variety of subjects. After all, I can see how people would think that in order to know so much about dog fighting, I would have

Opposite:
Dickie Freeman with George
(registered as Thomas), a great
son of Going Light Barney.

Norrod's Hemphill Maud, a good little red-nosed female with some good Wallace dogs in her ancestry.

The first litter of Bulldogs ever possessed by the author. The mother is Lightner's Peggy, a gift from the great breeder W. R. Lightner.

to be a dog fighter. On the other hand, there is an overabundance of critics who are perfectly content to label anyone a dog fighter on the flimsiest of evidence. Ownership of an American Pit Bull Terrier (or even a Staff or Bull Terrier, for that matter) will suffice.

Some of what I have to say about myself would hardly come under the category of bragging. For example, when I was five years old I remember how chagrined my father was when a playmate of mine (a girl!) killed a butterfly and I promptly burst into tears! We lived in the mountains then in a tough mining community and such compassion was certainly considered unmanly—even on the part of a young boy. For that matter, I can remember all through my childhood a number of times that my peers confided in me that I was "chicken-hearted" (*i.e.,* I had too much compassion for animals).

My father had to teach me to fight, as I was undersized and was a pacifist by nature. From my earliest years I loved all animals in general and dogs in particular. My father had always talked about his boyhood dog, a Collie named Jack. Jack apparently led a legendary life, whipping a sundry of

The all-time great breeder John P. Colby with one of the all-time great boxing champions, Jack Johnson, with a dog purchased by Johnson.

Opposite:
Stratton's Pokey, by Burton's
Dillinger out of Stewart's
Bronca.

Hammond's Samantha, inbred Bruno-Heinzl breeding.

The "sheep in wolf's clothing" with Wallace's Socks, a son of Wallace's Boots who was a son of Trahan's Rascal.

dogs, throwing a bull (I would have thought it was my father that was "throwing the bull", but Jack's exploits were also talked about by others!) and defending my father and his sister from threats from strangers, real and imagined. Naturally, I wanted a Collie, too, and I was eventually to have three of them. In the meantime I read all the Albert Payson Terhune stories on dogs (nearly always Collies who, like Jack, led heroic lives). I read those stories so much I wanted to be a Collie when I grew up!

Unfortunately none of my Collies, nor any of the others I knew (for I was now a "regular" at the dog shows), ever approached the legendary prowess of either my father's or Terhune's Collies. I began to look around. I took a serious interest in a variety of breeds before I finally discovered the Pit Bull. A veterinarian who was showing a Boxer at a dog show told me about the "American Bull Terriers". He said that they could whip any breed of dog and confessed that they were his favorite. When I was thirteen years old, I used money I had earned on a paper route to send to Louis B. Colby in New Hampshire for my first Pit Bull pup.

Later, living in Colorado, I became acquainted with W.R. Lightner, one of the all-time great breeders. It was through him that I got to know other devotees of the breed in Colorado. None of these fellows were into matching dogs for money, at least not on a regular basis. However, I saw numerous rolls in which the dogs were put down with no money at stake. In none of these rolls did I see anything that I could conceivably consider cruel. The dogs quite simply appeared to be having a marvelous time doing what they were bred to do—something akin to a fine athlete participating in his favorite sport. True, the dogs were "banged-up" afterwards, but they recovered quickly and seemed to suffer very lttle during their period of recuperation. They were obviously amazing animals, bred to dish it out and take it too.

It was not until I entered into military service that I began to see *bona fide* contract monied matches. I saw hundreds of matches during this time and I met dog people from all over the country. I met a variety of dog men and they were especially open and helpful to me. It was in this way that I developed the contacts that enabled me to have the knowledge of the breed that is normally privy to dog fighters. Thus, I was able to speak with the authority of a *bona fide* pit dog man. I had helped "school" dogs and I had helped some of the finest conditioners of all time train their charges for a match.

Well, then, does that mean I am willing to condemn dogfighting now as a cruel and barbarous sport? Sorry, but I don't have the hypocrisy to do that. To be perfectly candid, there is nothing cruel about pit fights. The cruelty of dogfighting exists only in the minds of those who know nothing about it. And, incidentally, isn't that why dogfighting is illegal? Because the laws were passed by people who know nothing about it? Well, of course, there are going to be many people who feel that they know *a priori* that dogfighting is cruel or that by its very nature the activity is cruel. Well, perhaps; but I don't think so. Then the solution is that I am a calloused person, right? Again, perhaps that is true, but

Tom II (age 22 months), son of George, great grandson of Barney.

Floyd Boudreaux with the famous dog Boze.

Greenwood's Oakie by Lonzo's Andy out of Lonzo's Faye.

Crenshaw's Champion Honeybunch, a great bitch and a great producer. The great dog Jeep was just one of her famous progeny.

you would have trouble convincing people who know me that this is the case.

I am almost ashamed to admit the deepness of the empathy that I have for animals and people too. I am unable to enjoy hunting or fishing—much to the chagrin of my youngest son who earns his summer money working on a sport fishing boat. I donated funds to stop the killing of baby seals and I have actually been a member of the Humane Society.

I am currently a science teacher and I am especially interested in biology. I am a Shakespearean buff and spend my evenings usually reading a variety of material. Articles I have written on various fishes have been indexed in the *Zoological Record* and *Biological Abstracts.* I am a strong chess player. I love classical music, opera and ballet. I am a member of the San Diego Zoological Society. I have been an assistant college wrestling coach and I have been a teacher at nearly all levels. At the age of 48 I jog regularly and am an avid tennis player.

To be perfectly candid, I have been bored silly writing these things about myself. I hope I haven't bored you too. I felt, however, that it was important for readers to know something of my interests and of the kind of person I am in order to evaluate my opinions and the validity of my information. To sum up: (1) I am not a dogfighter (an inaccurate term really—nobody fights their dogs—some *allow* them to fight!), although I have a fair knowledge of every aspect of the APBT; (2) I am generally known as a gentle person, both with animals and people; (3) I enjoy scholarly subjects and pursuits, but (4) I am athletically oriented too; (5) I love all animals and I vigorously oppose their neglect or any senseless cruelty imposed upon them; (6) I do not consider dogfighting (with Pit Bulldogs) cruel.

It's possible, I suppose, that dogfighting is just a "blind spot" with me. However, isn't it more likely that its detractors simply don't know what they're talking about?

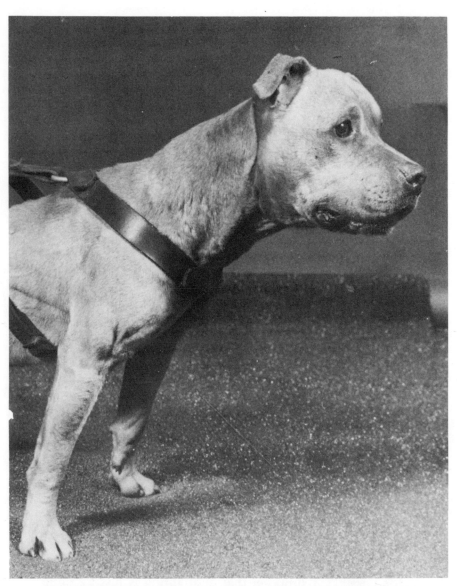

Garrett's Champion Jeep, a candidate for the greatest dog of modern
time. Sired by Finley's Bo out of Crenshaw's Honey Bunch.

Chapter 2

The Charms of the Savage Beast

I do honor the very fleas of this dog.
Ben Jonson

In view of the fact that I do not match dogs myself, there must be at least a few people who wonder why I put my neck on the line for dog fighters. A possible explanation could be that I am concerned that the matching of dogs will be stamped out. This would signify the end of the breed as we know it. The American Pit Bull Terrier would become another American Staffordshire Terrier and the thought of that is truly repugnant to me. However, it is my view that the fanaticism of pit dog men is such that dogfighting would continue even if it were made a hanging offense! For that reason I have little worry about the extinction of the breed. The real impetus behind my writings is my impatience with ignorance and its promulgation. And phenomenal ignorance abounds about dogfighting as a sport and about the breed that dominates it.

The very fact that there exist any fanciers of the breed at all would be remarkable. The fact that rabid fanciers exist in great quantity is nothing short of astounding! Just consider the fact that anyone owning a Bulldog is automatically a suspected dog fighter, an automatic pariah in normal society!

Surely that's like asking to be ugly! Obviously, there is something very special about Bulldogs to inspire such nearly irrational devotion.

Such dedication has not been restricted to morons and misfits (as some groups would like to have you think!) Most people would be surprised at the caliber of the average American Pit Bull Terrier fancier. Further, there has been no lacking of illustrious persons who have been devotees of the breed. John L. Sullivan not only raised the dogs, but he also wrote occasional articles about them. The Armitage book mentions Jack Dempsey's interest in the dogs and there are several pictures of Dempsey with several different dogs. Several modern pro football stars raise the breed and some of them have been to my home. Lest the reader be left with the impression that only athletes respond to the breed, let me hasten to add the names of Thomas Edison, Theodore Roosevelt and Senator Everett Dirksen to the list of those who were smitten by the charms of the so-called savage Pit Bull. In addition, I know a number of physicians, attorneys and research scientists who are true dyed-in-the-wool fans of the American Pit Bull Terrier. Some raise the breed and some only keep one at a time. The point is that they all respond to something in the Bulldog that they are unable to find in any other breed.

One of the things that is mentioned so often is the "lift" that one gets just from being around a Bulldog. Something about their natural enthusiasm and zest for life is obviously contagious. Strange as it may seem, one of the most engaging traits of the breed is its gentle disposition. I suppose one of the things that makes the good disposition appreciated so much is the knowledge we all have that the Bulldog asleep in our lap is the same dog that would fearlessly attack a bear or a lion and give him all he could handle!

I have discussed elsewhere the attributes of the breed. To sum them up they are prodigious strength, agility, an unusually stable disposition, intelligence, a comic personality, a quiet nature (quieter, in fact, than the Basenji) and, of

Left: Fulkerson's Aster. Sire: Menefees Max. Dam: Mason's Moll.
Right: Former world heavyweight boxing champion Jack Dempsey with two of his favorite Pit Bulldogs.

course, unbelievable fighting ability. Undoubtedly there will be many who will quite naturally be skeptical about some of these traits, as exaggerated claims are made by devotees of nearly all breeds. Perhaps knowing the origins of these traits may make them a little more believable.

Of course not all Pit Bulls have all the traits mentioned above. Some Pit Bulls may be barky and others may be stupid, but generally speaking the above-mentioned traits are typical of Pit Bulls.

One of the hardest attributes for many uninformed persons to accept is the good nature and stable temperament of the breed. However, it is easy to see how such a trait has evolved by the simple elimination of the dogs that didn't have it. Take into consideration, for example, the fact that in the pit the dogs have to be handled and ministered to many times in the course of a typical match. How much more difficult things would be if the dogs out of pain, fear, savagery or whatever, would be inclined to bite their handlers. For that matter, a dog that scratched to the referee instead of to the other dog would be a definite liability! Dogs that did not stay cool under pressure and make a definite discrimination between human and other animals were, therefore, systematically weeded out. Of course an occasional "man fighter" will turn up, but it is only the novices that will normally tolerate them. At a meeting that included some of the most knowledgeable pit dog men in the country, there was a general consensus formed that the Pit Bull (if so inclined) was perfectly capable of killing a grown man. When asked about the Pit Bull as a danger to humans I usually say that the Pit Bull is a thousand times less likely to attack a human than any other dog; however, if he *does* attack, he is a thousand times more dangerous! Just picture a Bulldog attacking a full-grown man with the same intensity as he does another dog. He would be impossible to beat off barehanded and he would quite likely bore in, grasp the man in the chest area and then shake. Even if the attack were terminated there (by outside intervention), a man could easily go into shock and die just from that! For that reason most Pit Bulls sign their own death warrant if they show any signs of aggression to a human.

Intelligence, again, is pretty much a matter of natural selection. Dogs that were able to learn tactics and strategy had a decided advantage over those that couldn't. Now we must be sure not to confuse intelligence with tractability. Some breeds, such as herding dogs, are specifically bred for tractability—the instantaneous obedience to commands given by voice, whistle or hand signals. Scott and Fuller (1965), however, found that one reason herding dogs did poorly in certain problem-solving tests was that they seemed to waste time standing around waiting for instructions or help. Hounds, on the other hand, which are not generally known for being tractable, scored quite well on the tests. With the bulldog, however, we can have our cake and eat it, too, for the breed is reasonably tractable and has an abundance of intelligence. Once a poor misguided soul stated the Bulldog brain was smaller than that of other dogs. Well, first of all, that just isn't true. The brain might seem small in bigheaded dogs compared to the size of the head; but the important thing is the brain-body size ratio, and on this basis the

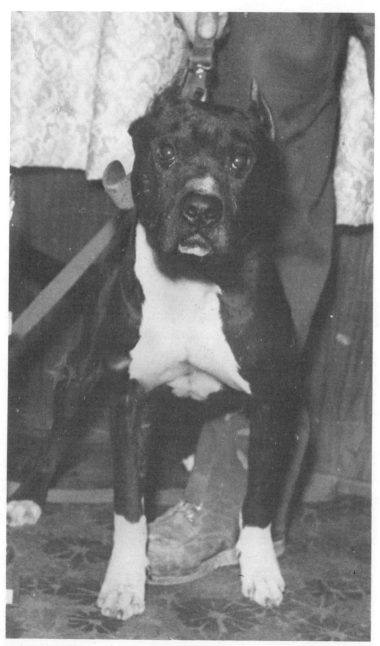

Champion Homer, a great dog and four-time winner; lost game to Jeep.

Petronelli's Pete of
pure Corvino bloodlines.

bulldog has a larger-than-average brain. Even if that were
not the case, we must remember that brain size alone is not
all that significant. Einstein's brain, for example, was aver-
age-sized. One of the largest brains on record was that of an
idiot!

The enthusiasm that the breed is noted for probably stems
from two selective pressures. Other things being equal, a dog
that would work well and actually enjoy training during a
keep would come into the pit in the best condition. Also, a
dog that enjoys fighting and has an absolute passion for it is
more likely to be a pit winner and thus be selected for breeding. This enthusiasm spills over into other areas and thus the
bulldog has a happy-go-lucky enthusiastic approach to just
about everything in life. This enthusiasm helps account for
his comic and sometimes roguish personality.

On the other hand, since many pit dog men were city
dwellers, it was advantageous to have a dog that was not so
hyper-active that he could not tolerate being chained up or
kennelled and left alone for extended periods. In the same
situation a barking dog would be a decided disadvantage.
Not only would it draw the ire of neighbors, but it would
also draw attention to the type of dogs our pit dog man was

40

keeping. (Contrary to general opinion, the general public of olden times was no more tolerant of matching dogs than is modern society.)

Strength and agility are obviously an asset in combat, so dogs with these characteristics would automatically be selected. A certain indestructibility was also a valuable asset that quite naturally evolved. No matter how strong or indestructible a dog was, however, if he lost interest or gave up in a fight he would naturally lose the contest and not be bred. Thus, gameness became an important quality. Gameness is actually an oversimplification that involves a variety of traits, mainly enthusiasm for fighting contact (winning or losing), endurance, resistance to shock and the ability to tolerate pain. This ability to tolerate pain has been thought by some to be a degeneration of the nervous system (of the pain sensors). I think a more logical explanation is that the Bulldog has developed a mechanism (or mechanisms) for overriding pain in a combative-type situation. Although a bulldog seems to have more grit than other breeds to resist pain in most situations, he obviously *does* feel pain and will yelp when stepped on just like other breeds. One reason some people think they don't feel pain is that they are so easily ministered to when injured. I think this attribute is the result of a selective process also. The dogs that could be quietly ministered to or even cooperate in their treatment were more likely to survive (and thus more likely to be bred). If a dog is subjected to a particularly punishing hold in battle, it will usually devise a defense to prevent the other dog from getting the same hold; the dog obviously feels something, although undeniably not as intensely as many other breeds. Recent studies have been done that indicate that higher organisms (including humans) have developed mechanisms for overriding pain under stress. Some substances referred to as endomorphines (or endorphins) have been isolated. I would suggest that the Bulldog would be an ideal subject for studies involving the production of these substances. I have a feeling the breed excels above all other creatures in its production!

At this point let us back up for a moment and take a look at all breeds and at the dog as a species. In this way we can view the American Pit Bull Terrier in perspective. First, the species. Most biologists believe that all breeds of dog are descended from the wolf. It used to be thought that the dog was an amalgamation of various wild dog species, but this theory has been largely abandoned. Some might still argue that the dog and wolf come from a common ancestor, but as I said the prevailing opinion is that we all have in our homes various wolves in all different sizes, colors and specializations. Some breeds are more wolf-like than others, both in appearance and behavior. That difference is explained by the history of domestication rather than by origin. The Bulldog, ironically, seems to be one of those breeds that have been "civilized" for a relatively long period of time. Conversely, the sled dogs are examples of a wolf-like dog. In their case not only were they evolved more recently from the wolf, but they also have been interbred with wolves, even in recent times.

The wolf, then, is a predatory animal that specializes in capturing its prey by running it down. It has outstanding endurance and toughness. The species has excellent sensory capabilities, especially auditory and olfactory, and it is a fairly intelligent animal. (The wolf is exceeded in intelligence, though, by a number of animals, including seals, elephants, dolphins and most of the primates.) The wolf was an exceedingly successful species but is being driven to extinction now (as are so many species) by the cancerous growth of human population.

Now let us look at our wolf descendents, our various breeds of dogs. A good point to keep in mind here is that most breeds are show breeds. That is, they have been bred for many thousands of generations strictly for appearance. Anything else you get will be strictly coincidental. (Of course most breeds have a lot of pap written about their usefulness at various activities, but these are mostly fanciful accounts, as are their official histories.) With the performance breeds there is more variety in appearance. They are bred for what they can do rather than for a specific type of ear, head, color, size and so on. Examples of performance breeds are herding dogs (Border Collies and Kelpies mostly), hunting dogs (bird dogs, spaniels, hounds and retrievers), guide dogs (strains of German Shepherds and Labrador Retrievers are mostly used for this), fighting dogs (Tosas in Japan, Chindus in Korea, Neopolitan Mastiffs in some areas and the king of them all, the American Pit Bull Terrier!) and racing dogs.

Notice that the various performance breeds take advantage of some aspect of the wolf that is superior to man. For example, the superior scenting abilities are utilized in the bird dogs and hounds to find game. Superior speed and endurance are utilized by the herding dogs. That same endurance added to formidability and toughness has, of course, been amplified in the fighting dogs. All the desirable traits are amplified by selective breeding for whatever activity is our concern. An important point here is that the performance breeds have been bred to love what they do above all other things. A Border Collie must be watched or he will sneak off and herd the sheep when his services are not needed. A hound would rather hunt than eat. A fighting dog, believe it or not, enjoys fighting contact. So that knocks the cruelty-to-animals theory into a cocked hat!

Like other performance breeds the American Pit Bull Terrier is quite variable in size and appearance and like other performance breeds, he is also very highly bred. His great strength and agility make him a natural for a variety of uses to man besides entertainment in fighting exhibitions. All the traits I have described play a part in his great appeal, but let's be honest. Those of us who dote on this breed appreciate its fighting ability. How many of us have picked up in our arms a small Bulldog we were walking on a leash when

accosted by an unleashed German Shepherd? Our concern is not for our little Bulldog who is eyeing the Shepherd intently as though it were his evening meal. Usually the other owner says something like, "Oh, he won't hurt your little dog!" We smile grimly and nod patronizingly, but how sweet is that inner smugness!

Opposite: Ronnie Anderson holding Champion Spade. Spade was sired by Hammond's Macho, out of Renee.

Reid's Dylan, by Reid's Sativa out of Reid's Babe. This dog
has ideal Pit Bull conformation, but his coloration makes him
look atypical.

Chapter 3

The Devil's Lap Dog

No one ever went broke underestimating the intelligence of the public.

H.L. Mencken

Recently I came across an article in which the Pit Bulldog was embraced by a Satanic cult of some type. The reason for the "honor" to our breed was not its supposedly evil disposition (as I might have supposed), but rather it was because they thought the breed was proof that the pig could be interbred with another species (presumably the dog). For some reason, this "proof" was important to their "religion." Well, I couldn't help chuckling to myself. There has been so much hogwash written about our breed! But at least this was obvious nonsense. Anyway, I thought it was. Sometimes, unfortunately, I am amazed at the apparent inexhaustible credulity of the general public.

The article, though, got me to thinking about two things. First, there is the tendency on the part of the media to project an evil image of the Pit Bulldog and then to associate him with various and sundry unsavory elements. As just one example, a television documentary on motorcycle gangs involved an interview with a man who had been primarily concerned with investigating these groups. The investigator ticked off an impressive series of evils that were suspected of the motorcycle gangs, *i.e.,* they were heavily into hard narcotics and were suspected of numerous robberies and the murder of a federal judge. However, he saved his most ominous tone of voice for stating that they were "really heavy into pit dog fighting". Well, I don't know how many of the other charges were true, but I can assure the investigator that none of these gangs are known on the pit dog circuit.

The other thought that struck me was that I had so often heard Bulldogs referred to as having a pig-like appearance. This has always astounded me, as there have been few Bulldogs that I thought looked in the least bit "pig-like". Of course maybe I'm kennel blind, having been around Bulldogs most of my life. It could be, perhaps, that our friends (the Satanists!) were confused and actually had the (English) Bull Terrier in mind because even to me those dogs do look a little pig-like, with their thick bodies and down-faced snouts. But, no matter. The statement has been made by others, too, with no doubt about what breed they were discussing. Actually, I've always felt that the American Pit Bull Terrier was a fairly average-looking dog. In other words they are pretty ordinary looking; some might even say they look like mutts. It depends on the individual dogs, of course, as some Pit Bulls are so dramatic in appearance that they are real "traffic stoppers". Others are quite homely. Again, we need to remind ourselves that the performance breeds are generally quite variable in appearance. To prove the point just compare bench show Beagles with field trial Beagles or show English Setters with field English Setters. Although there is variation in the American Pit Bull Terriers, there are parameters within which nearly all members of the breed fit. If we average out these variations, we get a type, theoretically an ideal type. When we start thinking in terms of ideals, a breed standard usually evolves since a standard is simply a description of an ideal type. One of the most interesting standards was devised by the American Dog Breeders Association. Several experts on the breed analyzed the physical characteristics of top winning pit dogs and from that devised a standard. It became the official standard of the American Dog Breeders Association dog shows in 1976 and reads as follows:

Basis for Conformation of A.P.B.T.

Experience with dogs, horses, human athletes, cattle, hogs and chickens indicates that for everything that lives and breathes there is an army of experts to tell you how that particular thing should *look*.

A lot of these experts seem to lack the ability to quantitatively distinguish one physical attribute from another. Most start with an animal they love and build a standard to fit, but some few are really awesome in their knowledge of which physical dimensions work best.

Those persons whose opinions on conformation have borne the test of years have, without exception, come from the ranks of the professionals who use the animals to make money. There are cattlemen who can look at two hundred calves and pick the ten best gainers by looking at their conformation. A year later those same calves bring more profit than their less well conformed brothers. Race horse men are the most knowledgeable conformation people you will meet. They all like the same basic things in a horse; although they claim to differ greatly, their differences are minute. As evidence, look at the bidding at a yearling sale when a foal of good conformation is brought in and compare it with the prices offered for an equally well bred foal with conformation faults. Good cattlemen and good horsemen judge conformation by what the animal is supposed to *do*. Cattlemen know from experience that they will lose money feeding narrow shouldered, hollow backed, longlegged calves. Horsemen know that shallow girthed, crooked legged horses with straight hocks seldom cross the finish line first, and that's where the money is.

Now, money doesn't give you good judgment, but it takes good judgment to hang on to it. You can bet that anyone dealing with cattle, horses or Pit Bulls for a long period of time professionally has been exercising good judgment.

Professionals look for an animal that can get the job done. Ama-

1

2

3

1) Snakeman's Nick has depth of chest for the endurance needed to make him a winner. 2) Ten's Pani has a stocky build made for punishment, but unimpressive conformation. 3) Irish Jerry's Pharoah is built for speed and strength; for conformation, the head might be a little large. 4) Wallace's Tiger displays nearly an ideal build. 5) Mongol Queen as a young pup and already showing well-balanced conformation. 6) Crum's Cremator, a winner both in conformation and pit contests.

4

5

6

51

Jack Williams' Clinker, one of the dogs of the Feeley line that Williams preserved intact (the line that eventually produced Dibo).

teurs, because they have no way to test their theories, wind up feeding their imaginations.

So let's get to the point of establishing a conformation standard for the American Pit Bull Terrier. If we are going to be forced by the laws and today's social standards into breeding a dog for looks rather than performance, in the interest of preserving the most extraordinary animal that man has ever created, let's take a good look at what the American Pit Bull Terrier is supposed to *do*.

His existence today was not because he was bred only for gameness. He was not bred only for power. He sure as hell was not bred only for his intelligence, loyalty, boldness, round eye, rose ear, red nose or his inclination for dragging children from the paths of speeding trains. He was bred to *win*. That's right folks; he was developed for competition.

The professional dogfighters have made him what he is, the professional dogfighters are improving him and when the professional dogfighters are gone, the real Pit Bull Terrier will gradually fade away. What we will have is something the amateurs have preserved that reminds us of the gladiators of old.

52

Thank God for the amateurs; professional dogfighting is a dying occupation. Preservation of this grand athlete that was bred to go to war is inevitably going to be in the hands of the amateurs. So, let's look to the profession of the dog in establishing our standard so that our grandchildren will at least see an authentic physical reproduction of a fighting dog.

If we start with the premise that conformation should reflect the ideal for the dog's usage and that this particular animal is supposed to win a dogfight, we come naturally to the question, what does it take to win?

Most of those who have backed their judgment with hard-earned money would agree on the following to some degree or another.

1. Gameness
2. Aggressiveness
3. Stamina
4. Wrestling ability
5. Biting ability

Note that only one of these qualities, wrestling ability, is directly related to conformation. One other, stamina, may be partly due to conformation but is probably as much reliant on inherited efficiency of the heart and circulatory system. Some people seem to feel that the shape of the head determines hard bite, but in practice, it seems there are a lot of other factors involved. Earl Tudor said that the great "Black Jack", who killed 4 opponents in 7 wins in big money fights, bit hard "because he wanted to bite hard." That about sums it up. Good biters seem to be where you find them regardless of the shapes of their heads.

When we talk of conformation we really only mean one thing—wrestling ability. This is the reason the American Pit Bull Terrier varies so much in conformation. His wrestling by itself is not nearly as important as the sum total of gameness, aggressiveness, bite and natural stamina, none of which are directly related to conformation.

Any dogfighter will tell you, "If you've got a game dog with good air, he's worth a bet." I might add, "If he can also bite, put a second mortgage on the house and take him to a convention." In other words, never mind what he looks like.

However, wiser men than I have said, "The only dead game dogs are dead ones." Also, "Under certain conditions most dogs will quit." I believe there's a lot of truth to that, and to reinforce the fact that conformation is important, remember that conformation and wrestling ability are very closely related and it's usually the *bottom* dog in the fight that quits. It's hard to stop even the rankest cur if he can stay on top. The dog whose muscle and bone structure don't permit him to wrestle on even terms needs more of everything else to win. He's always coming from behind. He frequently dies after the fight, win or lose. His career is short because each go takes so much out of him. So I believe that wrestling ability (and therefore conformation) is a very important ingredient in a fighting dog.

Our standard of conformation cannot be based on what someone who never saw a dogfight *thinks* a fighting dog should look like, but should be based on those physical attributes displayed by *winning pit dogs*.

American Pit Bull Terrier Conformation

Look first at the overall profile of the dog. Ideally, he should be "square" when viewed from the side. That is, about as long from the shoulder to the point of his hip as he is tall from the top of the shoulder to the ground. Such a dog will stand high and have maximum leverage for his weight. This means that standing normally with the hock slightly back of the hip, the dog's base (where his feet are) will be slightly longer than his height. Using the hip and shoulder as guides will keep the viewer from being fooled by the way the dog is standing.

Height to weight ratio is critical. Since dogs are fought at nearly identical weights, the bigger the dog you have at the weights, the better your chances. Hence, stocky dogs with long bodies, heavy shoulders and thick legs usually lose to taller, rangier opponents.

Nature usually blesses a tall rangy dog with a fairly long neck which is a tremendous advantage in that it enables him to reach a stifle when his opponent may have his front leg, to take an ear to hold off a shorter necked opponent, or to reach the chest himself when the other dog is trying to hold him off. The neck should be heavily muscled right up to the base of the skull.

Secondly, look at his back end. That's the drive train of any four legged animal. A Bulldog does 80% of his work off his hips and back legs.

A long sloping hip is most important. By its very length, it gives leverage to the femur or thigh bone. A long hip will give the dog a slightly roached backed appearance. Hence the "low set" tail so often spoken of.

The hip should be broad. A broad hip will carry with it a broad loin and permits a large surface for the attachment of the gluteal and the *biceps femoris* muscles, the biggest drivers in the power train.

The femur or thigh bone should be shorter than the tibia or lower leg bone. This means that the stifle joint will be in the upper one third of the hind leg. It is not uncommon to see dogs with a low stifle. They are usually impressively muscled because of the bigger biceps femoris, but are surprisingly weak and slow on the back legs because of leverage lost by the long thigh. A short femur and long tibia usually mean a well bent stifle, which in turn leads to a well bent hock. This last is a really critical aspect of wrestling ability. When a dog finds himself being driven backward, he must rely on the natural springiness of the well bent hock and stifle to control his movement. Dogs with straight or the frequently seen double jointed hock of many of the Dibo bred dogs will wrestle well as long as muscle power can sustain them, but if pushed, will tire in the back end more quickly and soon lose their wrestling ability.

Thirdly, look at the front end. He should have a deep rib cage, well sprung at the top, but tapering to the bottom. Deep and eliptical, almost narrow is preferred to the round and barrel chested. The rib cage houses the lungs which are not storage tanks, but pumps. The ribs are like a bellows. Their efficiency is related to the difference in volume between contraction and expansion. A barrel chested dog, in addition to carrying more weight for his height, has an air pump with a short stroke. He must take more breaths to get the same volume of air. Depth of rib cage gives more room for large lungs.

Shoulders should be a little wider than the rib cage at the eighth rib. Too narrow a shoulder does not support adequate musculature but too wide a shoulder makes a dog slow and adds unnecessary weight. The scapula (shoulder blade) should be at a 45 degree or less slope to the ground and broad and flat. The humerus should be at an equal angle in the opposite direction and long

Marshall's Tugger, a game and rugged half-Wallace dog (son of Wallace's Bad Red) and three-time winner, has a slightly larger-than-normal Bulldog head. Although difficult to see from the front, its shape is nearly perfect.

enough that the elbow comes below the bottom of the rib cage. The elbows should lie flat, the humerus running almost parallel to the spine, not out at elbows which gives a wide "English Bulldog" stance. This type of shoulder is more easily dislocated or broken.

The forearm should be only slightly longer than the humerus and heavy and solid—nearly twice the thickness of the metatarsal bones at the hock. The front legs and shoulders must be capable of sustaining tremendous punishment and heaviness can be an asset here.

The relationship between front legs and back should be, at first appearance, of a heavy front and a delicate back. This is because in an athletic dog, the metatarsal bones, hock and lower part of the tibia will be light, fine and springy. The front legs will be heavy and solid looking. The experienced Bulldog man, however, will note the wide hip, loin and powerful thigh which make the back end the most muscular.

The head varies more in the present day Pit Bull than any other part of the body, probably because its conformation has the least to do with whether he wins or loses. However, there are certain attributes which appear to be of advantage. First its overall size. Too big a head simply carries more weight and increases the chances of having to fight a bigger dog. Too small a head is easily punished by a nose fighter and is especially easy for an ear fighter to shake. In an otherwise well proportioned dog, the head will appear to be about two thirds the width of the shoulders and about 25% wider at the cheeks than the neck at the base of the skull. Back of the head to the stop should be about the same distance as from the stop to the tip of the nose. The bridge of nose should be well developed which will make the area directly under the eyes considerably wider than the head at the base of the ears. Depth from the top of the head to the bottom of the jaw is important. The jaw is closed by the temporal fossa muscle exerting pressure on the coronoid process. The deeper the head at this point, (that is, between the zygomatic arch and the angular process of the bottom of the jaw) the more likely the dog is to have leverage advantage both in closing the jaw and in keeping it closed. A straight, box-like muzzle and well-developed mandible will not have much to do with biting power but will endure more punishment. "Lippy" dogs are continually fanging themselves in a fight which works greatly to their disadvantage. Teeth should meet in the front, but more importantly, the canines or fangs should slip tightly together, the upper behind the lower when the mouth is closed. The eye elliptical when viewed from the front.

In general, such a head will be wedge-shaped when viewed either from the top or side, round when viewed from the front.

Skin should be thick and loose, but not in folds. It should appear to fit the dog tightly except around the neck and chest. Here the skin should be loose enough to show vertical folds even in a well-conditioned dog.

The set of the tail is most important. It should be low. The length should come just above the point of the hock, thick at the base and tapering to a point at the end and should hang down like a pump handle when relaxed.

The feet should be small and set high on the pasterns. The gait of the dog should be light and springy.

Most of the above relates to skeletal features of the dog. When we look at muscles, from the breeder's standpoint, it is much more important to look at the genetic features of musculature than those features due to conditioning. A genetically powerful dog can be a winner in the hands of even an inept trainer, but a genetically

Greenwood's Our Gal Sunday demonstrates the loose skin at the neck and nearly ideal set of the tail. Her back is a little long for the standard.

weak dog needs a good match-maker to win. Conditioning won't do much for him.

Think of bones as levers with the joints as the fulcrum and the muscles being the power source. The power being applied to the lever is more effective the farther away from the fulcrum it is applied. Muscles should be long, with attachments deep down the bone, well past the joint. Short muscled dogs are impressive looking but not athletic. A muscle's power value lies in its ability to contract. The greater the difference between its relaxed state and its contracted state, the greater the power.

The coat of the dog can be any color or any combination of colors. It should be short and bristled. The gloss of the coat usually reflects the health of the dog and is important to an athletic Pit Bulldog.

Above all, the American Pit Bull Terrier is an all-around athlete. His body is called on for speed, power, agility and stamina. He must be balanced in all directions. Too much of one thing robs him of another. He is not a model formed according to human specialists. In his winning form he is a fighting machine—a thing of beauty.

In judging the American Pit Bull Terrier 100 points will be possible for the ideal dog. The breakdown is as follows:

Overall Appearance	20 Points
Attitude Of Dog	10 Points
Head & Neck	15 Points
Front End Of Dog	20 Points
Back End Of Dog	30 Points
Tail And Coat	5 Points
	Total 100

Although this foregoing standard is the best ever devised for the American Pit Bull Terrier, in my opinion, a few comments might be in order here. First, if you were to attend a number of pit matches and attempt to select the winners by their conformation (assuming that you are able to interpret

This line drawing accompanied the original American Dog Breeders' Association standard and illustrates the points discussed in its text.

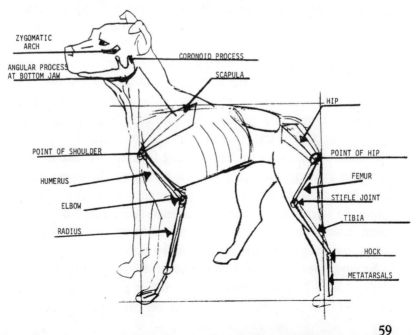

Johnson's Zebo, a seven-time winner. Far-from-perfect conformation, but one of the great dogs of recent times. He demonstrates that the real essence of the Pit Bulldog is in his mind and heart!

the standard with absolute perfection), you would probably be right about 50% of the time, if you were lucky! The point is that conformation most definitely has its limitations. The thing that makes a Bulldog a winner is very difficult to detect from the outside. What makes a Bulldog what he is dwells in his mind and his heart!

To avoid confusion, I need to comment on the statement contained in the standard that professional dogfighting is a dying occupation. Poetic license must be granted on a couple of points here, as I believe the statement was made with tongue in cheek. First, there is not and there never has been any such thing as a professional dog fighter. No one is able to make a living off the sport. In fact, just the opposite is true. If a man wants to be truly competitive in the pit dog game, he must keep a kennel of at least twenty-five dogs. He must raise scores of pups to get only one or two good prospects, so really it is just an expensive hobby.

Second, there is no sign of the sport dying out. Again, just the opposite is true. It has gone on for as far back as we can see, it is prevalent now, and it will continue to endure.

Getting back to other aspects of the standard, little is said about the ears of the dog. Should they be full drop, rose type or fully erect? Should they be cropped? I personally prefer a full-drop natural ear, if it falls right! However, the standard was written, as all standards should be, with function as a frame of reference. That's why ears were barely mentioned. In pit fighting it doesn't matter if a dog has full drop, erect or rose ears or whether they are cropped or uncropped. Oh, you can get some pit dog men to argue that a natural ear affords protection and you can get some to argue that cropping the ears takes the "handles" off the dog. But the very fact that you have arguments on both sides, however, illustrates the point that it really makes no difference. Whether you crop your dog's ears or not will ultimately be determined by what you think looks best.

The reader may not be aware of the fact that in certain countries humane-oriented groups have managed to make ear cropping illegal. As a matter of fact, my own personal view is that there is a mild cruelty involved in the recuperation from ear cropping, but not enough to justify yet another oppressive law! Anyway, in arguing for a similar law here the opponents of ear cropping often utilize the tactic of stating that ear cropping originated with dog fighting. Obviously this is supposed to evoke proper abhorrence. Unfortunately it just isn't true. As in so many cases, our critics should be asked to produce proof to document their wild stories.

Hard Rock, a winning pit dog, sired by Petronelli's Pete out of Carver's Miss Spike.

Chapter 4

Rogue's Gallery

*These were honored in their generations and
were the glory of their times.*
Ecclesiastes XLIV, 7

As I have said many times, the vast majority of American
Pit Bull Terrier owners never fight their dogs. Nearly
everyone, however, wants them from good game stock. And
why not? Gameness is the very essence of the breed and it
doesn't hurt your pride any to know that your dog was
descended from great ancestors. Moreover, the more people
that select and breed such dogs, the more likely we will be to
maintain or even improve the quality of the breed. With this
in mind I would like to tell the stories of some of the relatively modern dogs. As in the last book, worthy dogs will be left
out and for this I apologize. Unfortunately, space is limited
and some of the most reputable dog men operate in absolute
secrecy, never reporting any of their dogs' matches and
never offering dogs for sale or at stud. The result is that
these people never get hassled in the least degree, but a con-
comitant result is that their dogs never become famous. The
dogs, however, don't care and the owners are apparently
content with just a few people knowing of their quality.

There are a variety of things that determine whether a dog
will be an important one in the pedigree of future generations of good dogs. Some of these factors are discussed in the
following article.

Boomerang, one of the greatest of modern pit dogs, and may eventually outshine Dibo as a producer.

THREE BLOCKBUSTERS

Richard F. Stratton

(This article appeared in *Pit Bull Gazette*, November 1979)

In a small pit dog convention in a small Mississippi town several years ago, three dogs were matched that were to become legendary in modern pit dog history. They were Going Light Barney, Bolio and Boomerang. The three dogs were very close to the same pit weight, but they were never matched against each other. Barney and Boomerang both blew right through their dogs, winning with little difficulty. Bolio, on the other hand, had a rougher time of it, having to come up from the bottom to win. Bolio, thus, won the coveted "Best in Show" award. Boomerang went on to win five times in his career, three times winning a "Best in Show" award. Barney never won any such awards, but he compiled a higher win record than the other two dogs put together. (Bolio, having proven his gameness, was retired after his first match.) Unfortunately, Barney also suffered an ignominious defeat at a later match in Dallas. After being top dog for sixteen minutes, he was counted out in his corner. (The turn was called on the other dog.) This loss has made Barney very controversial—in fact, probably the most controversial dog in recent pit dog history.

There were other matches, you see, in which Barney had shown ample gameness. Twice he came up from the bottom to win. Twice he went over the hour mark. Once he came close to the two-hour mark. But there was still that quit in Dallas to produce a nagging doubt about Barney. His owner swore up and down that Barney was doped in that match. Others thought it was the unbearable heat that beat Barney. Still, a good dog is not supposed to quit—regardless of circumstances.

An alternative measure of a dog's worth is what he produces as a stud dog. Unfortunately, Barney has never been open to public stud, so little is known about what he has produced. The greatest known producer of our three blockbust-

A pit dog convention of the thirties. In the lower left is Bob Wallace, with Joe Corvino in back of him with his hand on Wallace's shoulder.

Wallace's King Cotton beat a winning dog so convincingly that he remained unchallenged and was retired to stud.

ers has been Bolio. We should keep in mind, however, that becoming a good producer is partly dependent on the number of times a dog has been bred. And I suspect that Bolio was bred more times than either Barney or Boomerang. Be that as it may, Bolio must already be credited as a great producer. Boomerang has been no slouch in that department either, as two of the greatest dogs in the country were sired by him.

When I say Bolio was probably bred more than the other two dogs, I am speaking hypothetically, as many breedings are kept secret and I am at opposite ends of the country from Boomerang. However, pit dog men have a penchant for breeding to the very gamest dog they can find. Deep gameness is the most essential quality in a pit dog and it is the most elusive trait to attain. For that reason, experienced breeders utilize the gamest dog to which they have access, with ability being only a secondary consideration. To some it may seem that breeding chiefly for gameness is a process that inevitably will lead to the deterioration of ability for the sake of gameness. That does not seem to be the case, for many famous producers of bone-crushing pit artists had little ability themselves. Thus, Wallace's Toney produced the immortal King Cotton, Bouncer produced Dibo, and Bolio produced the fabulous Chen Lang.

When a stud dog is evaluated for possible use, three main criteria are analyzed: the dog's breeding, the dog's own performance and what he has produced. Of course, if a dog has not been bred before, he can't be evaluated as a producer. However, if a dog is proven game and is from proven game parents and grandparents, his chances of being a producer are truly great.

There will continue to be arguments about the worth of these three dogs. In the final analysis, however, it is what the dogs produce at stud that determines whether they achieve lasting veneration. Bolio and Boomerang are already on their way toward immortality. Barney has only recently been bred and it will be interesting to see in the years ahead which of our three blockbusters is the most prized name in a pedigree.

What Bold Ruler was to horse racing, Dibo and Rascal were to the pit dog game. The following article told the story of Dibo.

THOSE SUPER-DUPER DIBO DOGS
Richard F. Stratton

(Bloodlines Journal, September-October 1976)

Thunder and lightning, fire and steel! Super strong and robust! That is the image of the Dibo-Rascal dogs, and while certainly not all the members of that line correspond to the image, it must be acknowledged that a number of them do, and the so-called Dibo line has been exceedingly popular for many years now. And those who study the pedigrees of their dogs take increasing delight at each appearance of the name Dibo (pronounced DIE-BO). For those who are interested in the history of the American Pit Bull Terrier breed, it should be mentioned that there are those who resist the idea of naming an entire strain of dogs after an individual

Left: Armitage's Mike, the dog made famous by Armitage's book, is found way back in most modern pedigrees. **Below:** The famous Dibo.

A pure Feeley dog of the thirties, the strain that produced Dibo.

dog, and who feel that the Dibo strain should be referred to as the Feeley line (while keeping in mind that, like nearly all the old-time lines, it is no longer a pure strain). Another name utilized at one time for the Dibo strain was "the Arizona dogs," as most of the original dogs were whelped in the Phoenix area. It should also be mentioned that there are also those who feel that the dawn of the Dibo era marked more a change in the efforts of the breeders of pit dogs than it did in the dogs themselves. Previously, the old-time breeders had always striven for gameness above all else and were content to allow ability to "turn up" of its own accord, but many of the post-Dibo breeders began to concentrate on ability and to merely hope that the dogs would inherit enough gameness to "carry" them. While the eventual results were the same, there had been a very definite change in emphasis. (In fact, old timers were wont to speak disparagingly of such breeders as "the modern Pepsi generation"!)

Those who call the strain the "Feeley line" do so to honor Con Feeley who was one of the few breeders praised in George Armitage's famous book Thirty Years With Fighting Dogs. Feeley had put together a family of dogs based on dogs he had imported from Ireland who were of the famed Old Family bloodlines. He owned a large saloon around the turn of the century, and rooms above the saloon were let out to rent. One of the tenants of one of those rooms was Jack Williams who, after Con Feeley's death, dedicated the latter portion of his life to perpetuating the Feeley bloodlines. A man named Bruce that had worked for Feeley and another one named Slattery also had a major hand in perpetuating

Hammond's Taffy, a dog
produced from the Heinzl
strain.

the old Feeley line. So it was that the Feeley strain was still intact
even after the Korean War. And the stage was set for the coming
of Dibo.

While most great dogs were the result of years of careful planning by dedicated breeders, Dibo was the result of a breeding
made by an amateur named Smith. It just so happened that the
dogs that he had in hand were absolutely top bred, and they were
of nearly pure Feeley bloodlines. Smith sold Dibo as a pup to a
man named Jensen who only wanted a pup as a pet for his young
son. The young boy named his new pup DUMBO (of all things!),
but later he tired of him and urged his father to get him a Collie.
(This was back in the days of the Lassie movies and of the debut of
the Lassie TV series.) Jensen contacted the great breeder Howard
Heinzl and offered to trade his Dumbo (Dibo) for a Collie. Now
Heinzl had mixed feelings about acquiring this dog. He knew that
both Bounce (Dibo's father) and Bambi (Dibo's mother) were good
dogs, but he had reason to doubt the quality of one of Bounce's
sisters. But Heinzl decided to take a chance, and got a Collie out of
the city dog pound for five or ten dollars, and traded dogs with
Jensen (who undoubtedly went home thinking he had pulled off a
great deal for himself!).

Even though Dumbo (Dibo) was two years old, he was a dedicated pacifist and ran loose at Heinzl's place, always staying out of
reach of the chained dogs (although he was occasionally bullied by

Mrs. Heinzl's Boston Terrier!). He followed Heinzl around as he fed the dogs and did the other chores.

When Earl Tudor (one of the most famous of the old pit dog men) visited Heinzl, he took quite a shine to Dibo, and Heinzl offered him any dog on the place practically, trying to get him to take a "good" dog. However, Tudor had faith in Dibo (he apparently got the name Dibo after Tudor got him), and took him home with him.

Well, the rest is history. Dibo went on to become a great pit dog, but his real contribution was his prepotency as a stud dog. He sired the fabulous White Rock, along with Tudor's Spike, Tudor's Jeff, and many other game dogs that were especially noted for outstanding ability.

The story of Dibo, besides being of interest to the modern Pit Bull and Staffordshire Terrier fancier for its historical value, is also instructive. Many modern fanciers (of Staffs and Pit Bulls)

Hammond's Teddy, a good pit dog that demonstrates the breed comes in nearly all colors, including black and tan.

confuse aggressiveness with gameness. Some of the greatest and gamest dogs have been easy-going animals like Dibo (whose name ironically has become a synonym for the fire-breathing type of Pit Bull!).

Most people are very interested in the Wallace dogs, as well they should be, as they reflect a lifetime of breeding selections by one of the most honest breeders of all time. Unfortunately, only remnants of the strain are left. The following article helps explain the reason for this state of affairs.

ADDITIONAL INFORMATION ON THE WALLACE BLOODLINES
Richard F. Stratton
(Bloodlines Journal, May-June 1976)

Some time ago, in fact over two years ago, I promised to give more information on the Wallace strain of the American (Pit) Bull Terriers. I had hoped to cover some of the other strains before getting back with this one; however, in view of the fact that I have been besieged by requests for information on the line (and meantime, I became bogged down with discussions of other matters in the magazine), I'll complete my dissertation on the Wallace strain now and get on to others at a later time.

The Wallace bloodline was originally based mainly on three dogs: Centipede, Searcy Jeff, and Wallace's Toney. Centipede was a pure Old Family Red Nose, owned by Dave Ferguson (who was destined to die a hero's death in World War II). Before his death, Ferguson was a trumpet player in a big name band, and had to travel a great deal. He would therefore leave Centipede with various trusted friends to care for him while he was on the road. Whoever kept the dog was allowed breeding rights, and, consequently, most of today's red-nosed stock has Centipede somewhere in its ancestry.

Wallace bred Penny (a Shipley bitch) to Centipede and got a litter of outstanding pups (Stinger, Scorpion, Spider, etc.) that came to be known as the "outlaws". Spider was bred to Searcy Jeff to

Above: Bob Wallace (taken in 1978). **Below left:** Wallace's Little Toney, named after the immortal Wallace's Toney who resembled this dog, and was the keystone of the Wallace bloodlines. **Below right:** Wallace's Searcy Jeff, originally owned by Dr. Hall, was described as the greatest pit dog of his time by all who ever saw him perform.

Wallace's Bad Red, one of the last of the pure Wallace dogs. An extremely intelligent and game dog.

produce a number of good pups, one of which was Madame Queen. Madame Queen was bred to Toney to produce King Cotton (who was discussed in the last article on Wallace). It should be noted at this point that, although the Wallace line was part Red Nose in terms of ancestry, the dogs themselves were mainly small brindle, white, or brindle-and-white dogs. It was this era of dogs of which Wallace was most proud. It was only later that Wallace began keeping dogs of the Old Family Red Nose to utilize as an outcross for his own bloodline. The latter-day Wallace line became an amalgamation of his old strain crossed in various ways with the Old Family Red Nose. They were larger dogs that were usually red in color and frequently showed the red nose.

During all these years (from the King Cotton era on), I had been close friends with the Wallaces. In those early days, however, I was not interested in breeding a particular strain: rather, I just appreciated a good dog. Consequently, many a good Wallace dog passed through my hands without ever being bred. Ironically, when I became interested in perpetuating the Wallace line, it was nearly gone. Wallace was old and infirm, and was not breeding dogs any longer, and those who had gotten dogs from him had polluted the line by crossing it to other strains. However, I received one male at this time, a solid red, copper-nosed dog called Wallace's Bad Red. The only other pure Wallace dog was Bob's own house dog, "Patches." By a strange stroke of fate, Red and

Right: Wallace's Spider, by Ferguson's Centipede out of Wallace's Penny. She was one of the foundation brood bitches of the Wallace line. **Below:** Red Duster, a remnant of the Old Family Red Nose line, bred by Jake Wilder.

Patches were to die within the same week of one another a few years later.

Patches (a very old dog) died of a heart attack, and Red perished in a tragic kennel fight with one of his own sons. Thus, in the wink of an eye, the last of the pure old Wallace dogs passed from this earth!

In the meantime, however, I had obtained, by courtesy of Bert Sorrells, a daughter of Wallace's Talking Boy. (Talking Boy was also known as Sorrell's Hard Rock, and was the sire of the now famous Dugan.) This little female (Sorrell's Cat Ballou or Riptide Rhoda) was bred twice to Riptide (Wallace's) Bad Red, and from these litters came Riptide Cyclone (Honey-bear), Riptide Talking Girl, and other quality dogs.

At this time, perhaps, I should explain the designation "Riptide". There were two or three other people in my area who became infected with "Pit Bull fever", and became interested in perpetuating the Wallace line. Since these gentlemen were marine biologists and oceanographers, and I, too, have been interested and involved somewhat in the studies of the sea, we hit upon the name "riptide" (an over-powering ocean current) to apply to the Wallace dogs we were trying to perpetuate. The "combine" that we formed may seem an unlikely combination of Pit Bull breeders, but it has proved at this date to be a felicitious one, and we all agreed not to sell any dogs until we had some measure of quality of our brood stock. A number of people have asked to buy dogs from me, and I have had to disappoint them. This summer we may disperse some of the pups for the first time, but only to people who are interested in perpetuating the Wallace line. (If we decide to release some pups, an advertisement will appear in *Bloodlines* later on this summer.)

Another breeding made with Bad Red was to Going Light Cindy, who was down from the Red Lady segment of the old Jim Williams red nosed line, and we thus have a line of Old Family Red Nose dogs to go with our Old Family (black nosed) Wallace dogs. It should be emphasized, however, that none of these dogs are strictly speaking pure Wallace dogs, but they are the closest thing to it alive today.

Finally, I would like to reiterate that it is not my intention to claim the Wallace line as the greatest ever. All strains produce

Wallace's Talking Boy, a seven-time winner and sire of the great Sorrell's Dugan.

good and bad dogs. The quality lines are only more consistent about producing good dogs. The main advantage the Wallace bloodline has to offer, in my opinion, is that, first of all, it is a relatively pure strain, and this in itself is a thing of value. Second, the line was originated and perpetuated by a man who was something of a genius at breeding Pit Bulls. And further, he was a scrupulously honest breeder who set the breeding down right and kept it straight. In this era of breeders who deliberately "scramble" pedigrees, that alone is worth a lot!

The following are individual dogs that either are already well established as important dogs in pedigrees or they very likely will be important in the years to come.

Alvin (Pit weight: 34 pounds)
One of the greatest dogs of recent times was a little spotted dog with the innocuous name of Alvin. Alvin was only matched twice, but he went against bigger dogs both times and demonstrated outstanding ability and gameness,

Above: The immortal Peterbilt, now owned by Mr. Doyle Reddick. He has near-perfect Bulldog conformation and was a veritable dynamo in the pit. Having demonstrated outstanding gameness, he is bound to figure prominently in future pedigrees. **Below:** Jessie Boykins, holding Pokey, a daughter of Dillinger out of a litter sister of Peterbilt.

especially in the second match which went in excess of two hours. Since he was a scatter-bred dog, conventional wisdom held that he would not be a producer of good dogs. Alvin, however, fooled everybody by producing many outstanding pit dogs, even when bred to a variety of bitches. The second and third-generation Alvin dogs have also demonstrated quality. Earl Tudor called Alvin the greatest dog he had seen in forty years. It is also interesting to note that while others were trying to get Tudor dogs, Earl Tudor was trying to get Alvin dogs!

Peterbilt (Pit weight: 41 pounds)

Peterbilt is the son of O'Brian. O'Brian himself was a great dog, coming up from the bottom to win in a match in which he demonstrated outstanding gameness and durability. Like Dibo, O'Brian's own performance has been overshadowed by those of his progeny. Dogs such as Peterbilt and Solomon are proving that O'Brian was a prepotent stud dog. At this date Peterbilt has won four matches, on one occasion going over two hours against a "bad" Bulldog. His most spectacular win was the time he was matched sixteen pounds uphill. For ten minutes the big 62-pound dog shook his smaller opponent like a rag, but Pete started coming up at the twelve minute mark and killed that big dog right in the pit in 37 minutes. (Apparently the owner of the big dog couldn't believe what was happening and didn't pick up his dog to save him!) What made the win even more impressive was that the 62-pounder had won twice at that weight in previous matches.

Jessie (Pit weight: 49 pounds)

Jessie came from a litter that produced great dogs such as Hank, a five-time winner, and Smith, a very game loser. While Jessie was not blessed with great ability, he compensated for that with great gameness and outstanding pit intelligence. He was a three-time winner and those who see his name in their dog's pedigree can be justifiably proud. Jessie was sired by Kephart's Tip and was out of Kephart's Suzie.

Blind Billy

Every man during the course of his lifetime has one particular dog to whom he is especially close. In Bob Wallace's words, "Blind Billy was 'kin' to Floyd Boudreaux". Howard Heinzl produced Blind Billy by breeding a daughter of Arizona Pete (Dibo's brother) to Dibo. Although he was blind, Bill was matched and gave an excellent accounting of himself. On his scratches he located the other dog by utilizing his sense of smell. He lost one match because his nose had been chewed on and he was counted out while searching the pit for his opponent; he could not find him because his nose was clogged up. After that Bill was retired to stud and he is in the pedigree of many of the great modern dogs.

Jimmy Boots (Pit weight: catchweight)

Jimmy Boots is generally considered one of the greatest of modern dogs. He was sired by Kennedy's Booger Red and was out of Uselton's Flo. To see this dog's greatness in true perspective, the reader needs to know that one of the most honored dogs of recent times was Bullyson. The only match Bullyson ever lost was to Benny Bob, his own son. Benny Bob, in turn, was beaten by Jimmy Boots in two hours and four minutes. Boots won over other rough dogs in matches ranging from seventeen to 48 minutes.

Hank (Pit weight: catchweight)

Hank was mentioned earlier as a brother to Jessie and Smith. A five-time winner, Hank is an impressive-looking dog and has already established himself as a sire of note. It was sometimes said that Hank did not outfight his opponents but simply dazzled them with crazy moves! A turn was nearly always called on Hank within the first two minutes and his scratches were a sight to behold! He would scratch in

A view of the famous "Pootch Patch", as Heinzl refers to his yard of dogs. From this "patch" came Dibo, White Rock, and a host of other great pit dogs, as well as some great race horses.

Floyd Boudreaux with his all-time favorite dog Blind Billy. This dog figures prominently in nearly all modern pedigrees.

a zig-zag style as though trying to avoid enemy torpedoes. Another time he would scratch to a neutral corner and then charge full bore on a bewildered opponent (and handler!) from the side! Actually, all these moves were simply idiosyncrasies (or "showboating") on the part of the dog. Hank won because he was the toughest, smartest and most durable dog in the contest.

Gator (Pit weight: 41 pounds)

Gator is the son of Boomerang. Boomerang is by Carver's Pistol out of Carver's Miss Spike (a daughter of Tudor's Spike). Gator is the product of Boomerang being bred back to his daughter (Miss Boomer) who was a granddaughter of Bullyson. Gator won three matches before he was two years old. (Most dogs would not even be rolled until they were two years old!) The last match was won over a particularly great dog and Gator had to demonstrate outstanding gameness as well as ability in order to win. He is the type of dog that is bound to be a producer.

Heinzl's Tinker (Pit weight: 48 pounds)

Tinker was a devastating dog and won four matches in the hands of several different owners. His last match was won with ease and was all the more remarkable because his teeth were worn down and he was nine years old!

Art (Pit weight: 39 pounds)

Art sailed through five opponents with incredible ease. Afterwards he was retired at stud (by a new owner) and was advertised as "Art, the dog with a heart". Despite being open to public stud the dog was stolen and although a three thousand-dollar-and-no-questions-asked reward was offered, he has at this date never been returned. It should be mentioned that the horse thief of olden days was popular in comparison to how pit dog men feel about dog thieves! The quickest way to get put out of the dog game is to get caught stealing a dog,

82

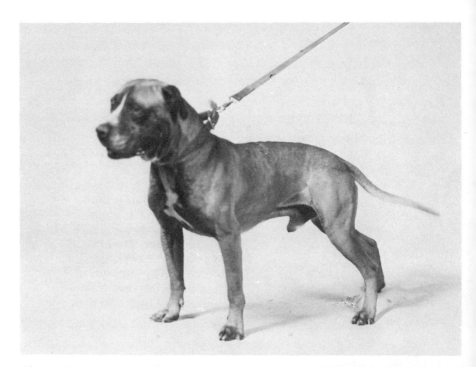

Above: Big as a bear and twice as strong, Burton's Hank! **Below left:** Gator, son of Boomerang and one of the greatest pit dogs that ever lived. He is highly valued as a stud dog today. **Below right:** Heinzl's Tinker won many matches in the hands of several different dog men.

Left: Tudor's Spike, one of the dogs that gave Dibo his reputation as a producer of devastating pit dogs. **Below:** "The Black Tornado", Grand Champion Hope was by Tombstone, out of Catfish, two great pit dogs in their own right.

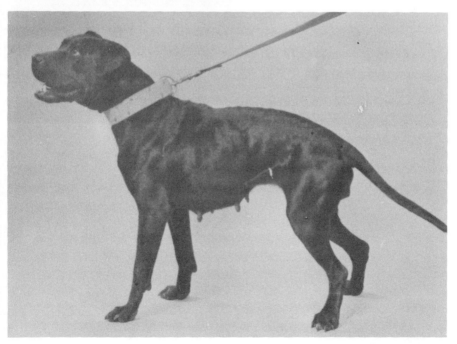

but sadly, certain misfits will still take the chance if a particularly good dog turns up. It is unfortunate indeed that Art lost his luxurious home and finished out his days with some lowdown dog thief who was unfit to even carry water to such a fine animal! Art was one of Eli, Jr.'s illustrious sons.

Tudor's Spike (Pit weight: 43 pounds)

Spike was one of the dogs that made Dibo such a famous sire. He was a rough and hard-driving dog that could actually break shoulders and have a dog helpless in short order. It is interesting to note that most of the dogs mentioned in this chapter have Tudor's Spike somewhere in their pedigree.

Hope (Pit weight: 39 pounds)

I suddenly realized that I might be in trouble writing this book! All the dogs I have mentioned in this chapter were males. Now that would get the feminists down on me very quickly. The truth is that there have been many great females too, and Hope is among the finest. She is a five-time winner and has been retired for breeding. Like her illustrious daughter, Hope's mother, Catfish, was a female with a winning record too. Catfish was bred to Tombstone (another winner) to produce Hope. At this date Hope is being bred to Hank and it will be interesting to see the quality of the progeny.

Having given a sampling of the modern pit greats, let us now turn our attention to an often-asked question. Are the modern dogs as good as the old-time dogs? My answer would be that they are better. In the old days it was easier for a particular dog to dominate because he was only drawing opponents from a relatively small area. In this era of rapid transportation a dog must face world class competition to prove himself an ace, for dogs will be brought clear across the country for the express purpose of beating him. Thus, there are few old-time dogs, indeed, for which I would trade a Gator or a Peterbilt!

Apache Red Baron, an Iron Dusty (Creed's Red Devil) dog.

Chapter 5

Another Glance at the Rearward Abyss

What is history but a fable agreed upon?
Napoleon

My first book was somewhat iconoclastic in several ways. One thing I did was to take on the conventional history of the American Pit Bull Terrier breed which decreed that it originated with a cross of the old Bulldog with a terrier. I countered with the idea that the Pit Bull was the old original Bulldog and that the Bulldog itself was the descendant of a fighting strain that dated clear back to Babylonian times. After the book was published I sat back and waited for the sparks to fly, but, amazingly, I received tons of letters agreeing with me! Many said that they had always felt that the American Pit Bull Terrier was the original Bulldog, and all others (of the Bulldog or Bull Terrier type) were simply show dog perversions of the original breed. The only controversy (or disagreement) that came to my attention involved the origin of the American foundation stock. Here is how it all started with a letter to *Bloodlines Journal* (November-December 1975).

To the Editor:
I have subscribed to *Bloodlines* and registered dogs with the United Kennel Club for a number of years. I have grown weary of

reading Mr. Richard F. Stratton's put-down and assassination of the American Staffordshire Terrier. My dogs are dual registered and as you know, many, many others are. The Staf and American (Pit) Bull Terrier are basically the same dog. I can't tell them apart, you can't tell them apart, and Mr. Stratton couldn't if he were put to the test. I don't see why we can't have more tolerance here. They are a great breed. I have been showing and training dogs for over 20 years. Recently, my dual registered Gallant Titan became the first of the breed in the world to win the protection dog title of "Schutzhund I." He scored 98 points out of 100, in protection. This was the highest score ever given to any dog by the judge, who is of European origin and with many years of experience. The Schutzhund (protection dog) work is extremely difficult and arduous and is based on courage and hardness. A dog must perform a tracking test, must retrieve over a 6 foot wall, pass an intensive obedience test with dogs and people around, and must be able to run 12 miles and then clear a 40″ jump. The dog must attack a man, defend himself and his owner and release the attacker upon command or automatically, when resistance ceases. It is a

The author judging a "fun match" conformation show in California.

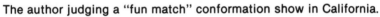

The author at age fourteen with the house dog Bingo, a pure Lightner dog.

complete test of a dog's stability, intelligence and fighting spirit. Through it, I found what my dog can do and what he is made of. The useless illegal perversion of dog fighting is not necessary. I don't believe Mr. Stratton could have much experience in training dogs. He suggests they can only be kept on chains or conditioned with an electric stinger. As a dog trainer, I know this is absolutely ridiculous and an insult to our great breed, besides being extremely misleading to the novice dog owner. My dog can go anywhere with me. He will not irresponsibly attack other dogs any more than he would other people. He has been trained and is obedient. On the other hand, he is a tough, courageous dog and has proven it. He represents the greatest breed in the best possible way.

Ralph Davis
Dallas, TX

The reader will notice that Mr. Davis did not question my treatment of the history of the breed. In fact he later wrote an article in *Dog World* which gave a view on the breed's history that concurred with mine. It was my answer to Mr. Davis (appearing in the same issue of *Bloodlines Journal)* that elicited a response from a third party that brought up questions of history. The following was my response to Mr. Davis:

First, let me say I am truly pleased that Mr. Davis' dog received the highest score in the protection area of his *Schutzhund* work. (Believe it or not, I do take pride in the achievements of the American Staffordshire Terrier, for I believe it to be very close to our breed!) However, I suspect the dog that scored second highest was a German Shepherd or a Doberman Pinscher, and it is well known among pit bull people that such breeds have no gameness worth talking about. Obviously, the *Schutzhund* competition is not a reliable means of determining a dog's gameness. I am really not quite clear on how I have "put down" or "assassinated" the American Staffordshire Terrier. I have said that the breed is in the process of evolving away from our breed and that they are, generally speaking, not game (and gameness, remember, *not* appearance, is the hallmark of the A.P.B.T.). But this is simply a statement of fact that can be verified by practically any pit dog man, and as a matter of fact, most of the older and experienced Staf people I know readily concede that, also. I also said that it was folly to change the name of our breed at all, and especially to Staffordshire Terrier, since Staffordshire is the name of an English county, and most of our foundation stock came from Ireland. Is Mr. Davis taking issue with this? If so, I would like to know the basis for his doing so. I don't have any experience at all in training dogs for competition because I simply don't have enough interest to do it. However, I have a deep interest in ethology, and I minored in psychology in college. In fact, I once trained rats to stack marbles in a tray, pigeons to play ping-pong, and chickens to dance the "jitter-bug"! So I have some idea of what animal training is all about. (And, incidentally, I recommend the training espoused in Dr. Whitney's books, *The New Dog Psychology* and *The Natural Method of Dog Training* rather than the force training methods utilized by most dog trainers.) I don't believe I suggested using an electric stinger; in fact, I said it would be akin to kicking a bird dog on point! Most Stafs do not have the urge to fight that most Pit Bulls do; yet most Staf people I know recommend keeping your Staf confined and on leash—regardless of his training. As I have pointed out many times, you are required by law to do that with *all* breeds in most parts of the country, anyway, so what is there to quibble about?

Now comes the question of history!

90

Right: Doyle Reddick with Tush, a winning daughter of the great little Alvin dog. **Below:** Reddick's Pedro, a three-time winner, grandson and look-alike of the great Alvin.

Haney's Grand Champion Little Roy.

ANOTHER POINT OF VIEW
L. Dillon
(*Bloodlines Journal,* January-February 1976)

In the November-December 1975 issue of *Bloodlines,* Mr. Ralph Davis took umbrage at Mr. Stratton's deprecation of the Staffordshire Terrier. I find that Mr. Stratton's misleading statements, made with all the infallibility of a Papal Bull, and without any substantiating evidence, equally irritating. In his reply to Mr. Davis, Mr. Stratton states:

"I also said it was folly to change the name of our breed at all, and especially to Staffordshire Terrier, since Staffordshire is the name of an English county, and most of our foundation stock came from Ireland. Is Mr. Davis taking issue with this? If so, I would like to know the basis for his doing so." As it so happens, Mr. Davis had not taken issue with this particular point, but Mr. Stratton, nevertheless, belabored him with it. It is pertinent to note that Mr. Stratton, in the July-August 1975 issue of *Bloodlines*, had twice repeated the gist of his above quote. I assume, therefore, that Mr. Stratton believes it to be of some importance.

I would be most interested to know the numbers of Pit dogs imported to the U.S.A. from England and Ireland, respectively.

Both of my parents were Irish, and I would be proud indeed to claim Ireland as the ancestral home of the Pit Bull, unfortunately, the claim will not stand up to inspection. Certainly, dogs were imported to North America from Ireland, but from where did the Irish Pit Dog originate? There is little doubt that many came from England.

Prior to the year 1840, there are numerous contemporary references in the English newspapers, magazines and books to the Pit Dog and the battles he fought. My own investigations through the National Library of Ireland, and other sources, indicate that in Irish magazines and newspapers of that period, such accounts are conspicuous by their absence. This fact causes me no surprise whatsoever, because the particular, unique, set of circumstances which generated the evolution of the Pit Dog, as opposed to the Bull baiting dog, occurred in one place only, and that place,—England. (I hope to be able to submit an article concerning these circumstances in the near future.)

Then, in the decade of the 1840's there was no interest in dog fighting whatsoever, for, in 1845, the staple diet of Ireland—the potato—was destroyed by the Potato Blight, a fungus disease imported from North America. Living conditions that year were appalling, conditions which were only to be exceeded the following year by a second potato crop failure. All of Ireland was in agony. Famine and disease rampaged unbridled throughout the land. Cattle, pigs, dogs, cats, rats and insects were eaten. It is no surprise that the original Irish Wolfhound became extinct about this time. (The current Irish Wolfhound is the synthesized creation of a Captain Graham.) There are records of families eating their starved, dead children, in order to survive. Women breast-fed their sick husbands to give them sustenance. The effects on Ireland

93

were catastrophic. The population dropped from nine million to four million. Of the five million souls lost to Ireland, half died of starvation and the other half emigrated. Many Irishmen could only afford the short journey to England, and in their countless thousands were absorbed by that man-eating machine, the Industrial Revolution. England, at this time, was the most highly industrialized nation in the world. Irishmen were to be found building roads, railways and canals; burrowing in the bowels of the earth for coal and iron; sweating in the iron foundries of the Midlands and the North. In such circumstances as these, the Men of Iron met the Dog of Steel.

For the workmen of the 19th century England, life was short and working conditions appalling. For example, in the coal mines, the grimy, naked bodies of men and women, hewed coal side by side for sixteen hours a day. Half starved, abject, naked infants, aged four and five, shackled by chains to loaded bogies, hauled the coal on their hands and knees—often up to their necks in water—along mine-shafts too low for them to stand upright. For such illiterate people as these, pleasures were few and limited, their whole existence was a fight for survival, and, thus, an abiding interest in the Pit Dog seemed inevitable, as he lived his life in the same invincible manner as they lived theirs—"Killed Sometimes, Defeated Never."

Dogs were rolled during work breaks, and large mixed crowds attended the matches held at weekends. A book would be needed to do justice to these early pit men, their lives, and their dogs. So, it will have to suffice to say, that Irishmen working in England, encountered the dog and were enslaved by his love of a fight, and his gameness. Those Irishmen who had 'made their fortune' in England, returned to their native land, bringing their dogs with them.

In 1855, one such young Irishman, believing, wrongly, that he had killed another man in a street brawl, fled from Walsall in England, back to Waterford, Ireland. Despite the haste of his departure, he still found time to bring with him, a 28 pound brindle bitch, named Lil, who was said to be 'the best bloody dog in the whole of Ireland.' Two years later, the same young Irishman imported from Walsall, a red dog, named Mick, a 40 pound pit winner. The offspring of Mick and Lil were snapped up by the men of

 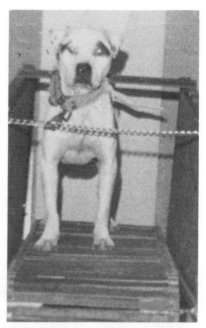

Left: Hammond's Nino, by Bruno out of Pinky. **Right:** Scotty C.'s Sultan, a game dog sired by Joker. Sultan is standing on a slat-type treadmill. **Below:** Throughout history, the Bulldog has earned his keep as a fighter *par excellence.* His is the epitome of the happy warrior. These were two Lightner dogs pictured in a roll more than forty years ago.

The great breeder Louis Sylvestri with the great little bitch, Goldy. This picture was taken over forty years ago at Sylvestri's luxurious home in San Francisco.

96

Waterford, and figured in many bloodlines. A sea captain, named Dolan, who lived in Waterford, brought several offspring of Mick and Lil on his voyages to the U.S.A.

George Stubbs, a well known singer in Vaudeville, toured the theaters of England and Ireland during 1880's. George's hobby was the Pit Dog, and when he was not working he was involved with his dogs. He was an engaging, lively personality, who brightened many meetings with his humorous anecdotes.

George was booked to perform during one Christmas week, in an Irish theater. Accompanied by a good quality Pit Dog, for which he had a sale, Stubbs boarded a train bound for Liverpool, England, and from there he would board a ship for Ireland. Stubbs recounted how the train contained many merry Irishmen, returning home for the festive season. In no time at all, his compartment was invaded by a number of these sporting Micks, who brought with them another Pit Dog. A challenge was made, accepted, and fought in the railroad compartment. Spectators were perched up in the luggage nets! According to Stubbs, he had a 'right royal Christmas.'

Subsequently, Stubbs made many trips to Ireland involving his Pit Dogs. He never married, devoting all of his time to his dogs, and he eventually became the doyen of pit men in the mining area of North Eastern England. He produced a fine strain of sporting dogs which he exported to all parts of the world—some of his best customers being Irishmen. The foundation of his dogs came from the cities of Birmingham and Newcastle. Incidentally, Newcastle is in North Eastern England, and Walsall and Birmingham are cities in the county of *Staffordshire, England.* Stubbs was active with his dogs, until the outbreak of World War II. He died at an advanced age in Norton-on-Tees, N.E. England.

Mr. Stratton has also claimed that the Staffordshire Bull Terrier is not game. I wonder how many Staffordshire Bull Terriers he has seen in Great Britain? Recent investigations show that dogs are no longer fought in Waterford, but are used for Badger drawing. Because these dogs are not allowed to fight in Southern Ireland, is it fair to assume that the dogs are no longer game?

The men who are currently pitting their Staffordshire Bull Terriers in Belfast, Northern Ireland, would consider the statement laughable, and tantamount to their asserting that the Pit Bull is

Clark's Jerry, a dog belonging to Harry Clark back in the twenties.

not game. The record well shows that none of the strains of fighting dogs have a monopoly on gameness, and to condemn any one of these strains is not only unfair, but unnecessary.

And this was my reply.

REPLY TO MR. DILLON
Richard F. Stratton

(*Bloodlines Journal,* March-April 1976)

In reading Larry Dillon's article in the last issue of **BLOODLINES,** I became so engrossed in his tale of Irish sufferings that I nearly forgot for a time that it was my hide that he was nailing so neatly to the wall. As a reminder to readers, Mr. Dillon took me to task for (1) misleading people into thinking that the ancestral home of the APBT was Ireland, (2) casting doubt upon the gameness of the Staffordshire Bull Terrier, and (3) he even castigated me severely for belaboring Mr. Ralph Davis with a point he had not even brought up. Well, regarding the last part, perhaps readers will recall that Mr. Davis had complained that I had been guilty of deprecating the American Staffordshire Terrier. So I simply restated what I had actually said about the breed and tried to put my remarks into perspective. I had not thought that any of that was difficult to follow.

Regarding the ancestral home of the APBT, those who read my book will note that I state that no one nation can make a sole claim to the breed. In any case, I have never tried to claim Ireland as the origin of the breed; however, I have indicated that the bulk of our foundation stock came from there. And it is hard for me to see how anyone could take issue with such a statement, for the importations are well known among Pit Bull people, and have been mentioned in various old publications such as the Police Gazette, the Dog Fancier, and Pit and Pal (not to mention old issues of Bloodlines). Various dog books such as the Armitage and Colby books have also mentioned the importations from Ireland. I'll grant that there were undoubtedly a few importations from England, too, but my conversations with dog men whose lives extended back into the last century indicate that dogs were available from several countries, but the Irish dogs (and game chickens) were always the preferred stock because they were so renowned for their gameness. Incidentally, the great breeder William J. Lightner once told me that his father and uncle had imported dogs from Ireland before our Civil War.

As for England being the origin of the Irish pit dog, I wouldn't argue with that, but it is an unproven theory—especially if we are designating England as the origin of the breed. It should be noted that 15th and 16th century artists, such as the Flemish painter Rubens and the Dutch painter Veldes, have depicted dogs utilized in boar hunts that look every bit like a modern APBT. (Also, the Denlinger book on the Pit Bull contains a copy of an old woodcut that shows Spanish Bulldogs that also look just like ours). The old literature of other countries may not refer to our dogs by name, but it does contain references to "bear dogs" and "bull biters." And references to fighting dogs are known from ancient civilizations, and artifacts that contain representations of dogs looking very much like modern Pit Bulls have been found. So the question is: at what precise point do we declare that ancient fighting strain

Clemmon's Brendy, a good little bitch that appears in the pedigree of many good dogs.

to be our breed? I don't propose to answer that, but I do think we can smile in amusement at the old tales about our dog originating from a cross of the old Bulldog with a terrier.

As for the Staffordshire Bull Terrier being a game breed, we must remember that the Stafford is merely the show counterpart of the English pit dog. (If there are any *bona fide* pit dogs left in England, I seriously doubt that they are called Staffordshire Bull Terriers by their owners). The Staffords in England may be game as Mr. Dillon implies but it does seem unlikely inasmuch as the individuals presently in this country are largely from imported stock (second or third generation). Even Mr. Dillon, apparently, does not try to claim any degree of gameness for our "resident" Staffords! As for the present-day Irish pit dog men who would consider my statements about the Staffordshire Bull Terrier to be so laughable, I am told by Mr. Al Brown of Arizona, who has been in recent contact with such men, that they refer to their dogs as "pit terriers" and that they no more resemble Staffords than did the imports of a hundred years ago!

Although it may not seem like it, Mr. Dillon and I are "kindred spirits" of sorts, for we both are sufficiently interested in the history of the breed to do personal research. It is our methods of investigation that differ somewhat. It is my view that Mr. Dillon relies too heavily on old public writings. This may not be the best course in trying to research a unique breed whose owners have traditionally endeavored to keep its very existence a secret, and who have, on occasion, deliberately misled "outsiders." The result of this situation has been that the public view has always been completely off base. Just imagine how completely misled some future historian would be if he tried to rely on the references to our breed that have appeared in the papers over the last couple of years!

John Fonseca as a young man with his pure Colby dog Tinker. Mr. Fonseca is still breeding the Colby line, and is a great authority on the breed as well as an elegant gentleman.

Chapter 6
Echoes and Reflections

*Truth forever on the scaffold. Wrong forever
on the throne.*

Lowell

My writings on dogs have appeared in a variety of publications such as *Bloodlines Journal, Sporting Dog Journal,* and *Pit Bull Gazette.* I am including some of them in this chapter. Along with my own, I am also including a few articles by other authors. I would have included more, for many worthy articles have appeared; however, as my wife pointed out, the book is supposed to be by me!

This first article is special to my family. Belle was our favorite house dog of all time. She had been given to me as a pup by Bert Sorrells. She was taken from us all too soon in the prime of her life by a botched up hysterectomy. About the time of her death, the publishers selected her picture for the cover of my first book. It was small consolation to my family, but it was a nice memorial for a worthy dog.

AU REVOIR, BELLE
Richard F. Stratton

(*Bloodlines Journal,* March-April 1977)

She was so much a part of our family that even now, a year after her death, it is difficult to write about her without feeling a touch of sadness. But she deserves to be remembered and written about. She was the one that finally won over my wife to the breed. When we were first married over 20 years ago, my wife had a delightful Shetland Sheepdog, and I had two Wallace-bred American Pit Bull Terriers. Sable (my wife's dog) was an unusually intelligent animal who had been hand raised and taught to do a lot of cute tricks. Quite frankly, he was loaded with personality and was one of the smartest dogs I've ever known. (the *very* smartest dog I knew was an APBT!) My Pit Bulls, on the other hand, were kennel raised and got precious little attention from me, as I was busy with my studies in college. Being raised as they were, the only trick they could do was to make a dog disappear! (And I was pretty sure that my wife wouldn't care for that trick!) Round one went to the Shetland Sheepdog.

Later on when my boys were babies, we had a Wallace-bred Old Family Red Nose dog named Sam as a house pet. He was great with the boys, and I recall how my father-in-law was highly impressed with his deportment. However, an incident in our town in which a German Shepherd killed a small child entrusted to him so horrified my wife that I knew she would never rest easily with Sam as a house dog. So I got the family a Dachshund pup, and poor Sam was relegated to the kennels. Round two went to the Dachshund.

Finally, when the boys were older, I brought home a little pied pup with a pink nose. The boys named her "Belle", and doted on her. By the time she was grown, she had won my wife over completely, as she acknowledged that Belle even outshone the memories of her beloved Sable. For Belle could do tricks, too, and many of them were self-taught! In addition, she had the typical Pit Bull zest for life that is downright contagious. Her excitement and enthusiasm made every outing an adventure for her and somehow less mundane for the rest of us. She was a joyful companion, and she brightened our days.

Not everything was all roses, of course, during her time with us. For one thing, she had a penchant for killing skunks, and we soon learned where the skunks lived, or at least used to live. We also found a chemical that killed skunk odor even better than tomato juice. As bad as she was with skunks, she was amazingly good with other dogs. We were able to take her with us and allow her to run

Left: The author's dog, Belle, investigating—and enlarging—a hole at the ocean's edge. **Right:** Belle clearing debris out of the water. **Below:** Red Lacy's dog who herded sheep and babysat children.

John Stratton as a young boy with Dolly (as a young pup).

off lead in the areas in which such things were allowed, and she never bothered a dog that didn't make the terribly self-destructive mistake of jumping her first.

One of her favorite romping places was at the beach where she liked to swim out and do battle with the waves. I have noted that retriever trainers are careful never to start out their water dogs in ocean water. They are afraid that their dogs may swallow some salt water and lose their incentive for swimming. But Belle swallowed half the ocean and never lost *her* enthusiasm. Freshwater lakes and streams must have seemed a little tame to her after "surfing" in the ocean, but she managed to have fun in these areas, too. She was obviously an ecologist at heart, as she retrieved all the floating debris from lakes, dropping it at our feet for us to put in the trash.

In a bay area near our town, dogs are allowed to run loose legally, and it is here that people bring all manner of dogs to romp. It is a delightful area, and is perfect for training retrievers, bird dogs, and Beagles. But, whenever we were there with Belle, she stole the show from all the rest. People seemed only to have eyes for her, and all the other dogs were neglected. The owners of other dogs even pestered us, wanting to know what kind of dog she was and where they could get one like her.

Well, I'm not sure that there are many like her around, but we have a puppy now that sure looks like her and shows lots of promise and personality. Although this new pup will replace Belle as our house dog, our family, and my wife in particular, will always remember Belle as a very special dog.

BOB WALLACE

Richard Stratton

(*Pit Bull Gazette*, March 1977)

It's funny how erroneous impressions tend to persist in spite of
what anybody says to try to dispel them. Two such fallacies
regarding Bob Wallace immediately come to mind. One is the idea
that Bob Wallace and Bob Hemphill were partners in the breeding
of their dogs. Some people even refer to the Wallace-Hemphill
bloodline. The other is the notion that Wallace was primarily a
breeder of the Old Family Red Nose line. It is true that Bob was
an admirer of the old red nosed strain, but his original line consisted of little bundles of dynamite that were generally quite variable
in color.

Of course, even though Bob's original line didn't show it, they
carried a substantial amount of the Old Family Red Nose blood.
Since Bob had always considered Jim Corcoran to be perhaps the
greatest breeder of all time, he selected as his foundation bitch, a
game little Shipley bitch named "Penny". (The old time Shipley
blood was descended directly from the Corcoran line.) "Penny"
was bred to "Centipede", one of the great red nosed dogs of his
day. From this breeding came "Stinger", "Scorpion", and
"Spider"—all of them game and rugged pit dogs. "Spider" was
bred to "Searcy Jeff" (generally considered the greatest pit dog of
his day) to produce "Madame Queen".

When "Searcy Jeff" was owned by Dr. Hall, he was matched into two Lightner dogs, and won handily over both of them. However, the losing dogs showed such gameness that Joe Corvino of
Chicago obtained a litter sister to these dogs and bred her back to
"Searcy Jeff". A pup from this breeding was also sent back to Dr.
Hall. Wallace later obtained a grandson of this little bitch, and he
named him "Toney". "Toney" became famous for one of the
gamest scratches of all time (at Rulesville, Mississippi), and he
later was bred to "Madame Queen" to produce "King Cotton". It
would be instructive at this point to mention the colors of the dogs
we have been talking about. "Penny" was red with a black nose,
"Centipede" was red with a red nose, "Spider" was red with a
black nose, "Madame Queen" was a brindle with a black nose,

and "King Cotton" was white with a black nose. We see, therefore, that the Wallace line did not show the red nose even though the Old Family Red Nose strain was an important component of the line. We find that the Wallace bloodline was an amalgamation of the Corcoran (Shipley), Lightner, and the Old Family Red Nose strains.

Many years later, Wallace felt that his bloodline was losing some of its vigor and bite, so he analyzed the options for an outcross. In those days, strains were kept more pure than they are now, and breeders dreaded the time that was bound to come when they would have to think in terms of breeding to an outside strain. Wallace especially dreaded the idea of a rank outcross in which there were no common bloodlines. Finally, he had the inspiration to utilize the Old Family Red Nose line, and it was at this time that he obtained what was left of that old strain and kept it pure to utilize as a cross for his main line.

When I first visited the Wallace's seven-acre country home, the red nosed dogs comprised only a small portion of the dog aggregate, and they were kept in their own section of the place. And a beautiful place it was too. I was especially impressed with how the dogs were kept. There were kennel runs and large spacious pens for puppies, but the adult dogs were kept on pulleys attached to cables. I had always felt that the cruelest aspect of any activity involving any breed of dog, was the confinement that was necessary for keeping a large number of dogs; however, the Wallace dogs on

Lightner's Bucksy, a typical Lightner dog in a picture taken in 1919.

Left: Pete Cain's Dusty. Dusty appeared in the "Tall Tales" chapter of *This Is the American Pit Bull Terrier.* He was a pure Lightner dog. **Right:** Lightner's Peggy with two kittens for which she was a foster mother.

their cables were the least confined kennel dogs I had ever seen. A lot of thought went into Bob Wallace's total set up, from the cable system to the specially designed dog houses. Such attention to detail was typical of Wallace's commitment to the breed.

Although, as previously mentioned, Bob Hemphill was not a partner of Wallace's, he wrote the following about him in the January 1953 issue of *Pit Dogs:*

> *"In my humble opinion, Bob (Wallace) will go down in pit dog history as one of the all time great breeders. Bob is a perfectionist, a breeder that plans his breedings years ahead and leaves nothing to chance to establish the correct pedigree of any animal he uses. Impatient with those who are never sure or are careless with the recorded breeding of their dogs, Bob's word is his bond. I would unhesitatingly accept his version of any breeding on any dog, no matter how controversial the known pedigree might be. Educated, intelligent, a successful businessman, a sportsman who will meet any man and lay his money on the line, Bob would be a credit to any sport where sportsmanship prevails."*

HAPPY NEW YEAR TO MR. ROBERT FOSTER (BOB) WALLACE

Jean Carpenter

(*Pit and Pal,* January-February 1979)

We want to start the year by honoring Mr. Bob Wallace! Mr. Wallace is a household word to Pit Bull Owners old and new. He is also known for the "Old Family Red Nose" strain, his honesty, and for being out-spoken when called for. Mr. Wallace played football and boxed in his younger days and never lost interest in the Pit Bull Dogs. No matter how many "Pits" he had on his yard, (sometimes 50-60) he always had a couple of good bird dogs, as his second love was quail hunting. Mr. Wallace worked for Libby-McNeil-Libby as sales manager until liquor was legalized and he became connected with a well known Kentucky Distillery in 1942. He left the distillery and opened his own retail stores in the Little Rock, Arkansas area. He owned and operated five retail stores until his retirement in 1960. He made his living from his profession. His dogs were a hobby, not a way to make money. Mr. Wallace said he sold a total of 10 Pits in his life, but he had placed some in the hands of Fanciers who would recognize their true value and give them a chance to prove it.

Mr. Wallace was born in Van Buren, Arkansas, May 28th 1904. He received his first Pit Bull dog at the age of four from an Aunt. Due to a "no-money" match between his Pit and one of his father's coon dogs (guess who won) his father found a new home for the Pit. Mr. Wallace not being a quitter had many Pits during his teens. When he was 13 he met Mr. Ben Flannery, a well-known dog fighter of his era. Mr. Flannery told him all about dog fighting and Mr. Wallace really got 'The Pit Dog Fever'. After he became grown and married to the lovely Doris Dewitt Wallace, they bought a pup from the "Dugans Pat bloodline". His name was "Spike". This was the Pit he had his first money match with and won in 39 minutes, over Charley Beckels' "Pat" out of Paris, Ark. Spike broke Pat's hind leg and was picked up. Mr. Wallace did not condition and handle all the dogs that he fought. This was true of his good friend, Mr. Joe Corvino, whom he considers the best breeder of his day. Mr. Wallace said that dog breeders and

110

Slim Emerson (left) and Joe Corvino with Thunder after he won over Corvino's Smilin' Jack in the late thirties. Corvino later purchased Thunder.

dog fighters were two different categories and only a few had the time to do both. Mr. Wallace and Mr. Corvino never met "across the pit" but on one occasion, "King Cotton" (Wallace breeding) and "Davidsons' Blackie" (Corvino breeding) were matched and King Cotton won in 1 hour and 44 minutes. Mr. Wallace said that Mr. Corvino was a top dog man, a breeder second to none and a credit to the Game.

The man who helped Mr. Wallace start his bloodline and contributed the most to his success was Mr. Oscar (Chuck) Hufft of Bossier City, Louisiana. Chuck gave him "Penny", a Shipley red bitch for his foundation bitch. Mr. Wallace said Chuck was known to all Pit Dog breeders and fighters as a man of honor, good as his word, truthful and honest. A group of traits hard to find in any man. Mr. Hufft hung up his 'breaking sticks' in the mid 40's. He is now eighty-four years of age and still has a couple of good Pits in his back yard.

I asked Mr. Wallace to compare today's dog men with yesterday's dog men. He said it would be difficult, but all in all, they compare favorably except for one small detail, the desire to short cut time-tried conditioning methods and the use of chemicals, pharmaceuticals and medicine today as compared to the old time "natural methods". This has resulted in fewer dogs being put in top shape for long matches. But, they seem to have more "chewum up and spit'um out" type of dogs today. Mr. Wallace sometimes refers to the younger men as the "Pepsi Generation".

111

Above: Wallace's Dude, a white-headed, red-nosed dog that figured prominently in the latter day Wallace strain. **Left:** Wallace's Bullet with Howard M. Hadley's son-in-law. Bullet was sired by Searcy Jeff and was a brother to Wallace's Trigger. **Right:** Wallace's Trigger, better known as Popeye, was the Wallace house dog for many years. He was by Searcy Jeff out of Flash, a daughter of Searcy Jeff.

Mr. Wallace said the greatest dog he ever bred was never fought for money. He was a pure red-nose named ("Curly") Wallace's "Red Brave", pit weight 48. He three dogged him and nearly killed him. He could bite, wrestle, and he was a smart fighting dog. He nearly died from the gameness test and Bob promised Mrs. Wallace that he would never fight him again, so he became the "House Pit." The Wallaces' house Pit today is a line bred "Rascal", Corvino dog named "Wallace's Little Joe", a red and white, three year old that travels with them.

Mr. Wallace, we wish for you: GOOD HEALTH AND LOTS OF HAPPINESS IN THE NEW YEAR AND "KEEP SCRATCHING".

THE REVEREND HEINZL
Richard F. Stratton

(Bloodlines Journal, March-April 1977)

It has been my good fortune and pleasure to have known some of the great all time breeders of the American Pit Bull Terrier. One of the most engaging is Howard Heinzl of Tempe, Arizona. Howard's reputation as a breeder of quality dogs is unassailable, but he is also known for his entertaining wit. As I've always said, you have to "listen quick" when Howard talks because he talks in such a quick and concise way he gets a normal hour's dissertation into about five minutes talking time. Since his experience with the dogs goes back to the days of Con Feeley and George Armitage, he has many fascinating and entertaining stories to tell about the great old dogs and their owners. My wife thinks that he is funnier than Burt Reynolds—and better looking too!

For some reason that I'm not sure about, Howard is often affectionately referred to as the "Reverend Heinzl" by other dog men, and he often signs his letters in that way. Perhaps he attained the title from the narrow path that he exhorts APBT fanciers to follow. He has absolutely no patience with those who neglect their dogs, and he is not shy about letting anyone know about it. He practices what he preaches, too. His dogs are religiously picked up after twice a day, are kept free from fleas and flies, and are provided clean and comfortable quarters. Personally, I think we need

113

The master breeder and great wit Howard Heinzl.

more reputable breeders like Howard to put pressure on would-be
dog men who want the dogs, but are lazy about caring for them.
Howard has also been very interested in dog nutrition, and, of
course, provides his own dogs with a scientifically-oriented diet.
In addition to Pit Bulls, Howard raises thoroughbred racing
horses but his prime interest is always the good old American Pit
Bull Terrier.

Howard names Con Feeley, Rip Torn, John P. Colby, and Earl
Tudor as the top dog men that he has known in his life time, and
as it turned out, it was a cross of the Colby and Feeley bloodlines
that produced Dibo. Dibo became famous as the most prepotent
stud dog of modern times. Heinzl refers to his old Dutchess dog as
the best Pit Bull he ever owned or saw, but he is probably more
famous for his association with Dibo and the immortal White
Rock.

Another dog that is brought to mind when you think of Howard
Heinzl is Gringo. Gringo sired some great dogs, and, consequent-

Above: Orday's Smokey was by Colby's Dime out of Colby's Cheyenne.
Right: Another shot of John P. Colby and Jack Johnson with "Flub-Dub".
Below: John P. Colby's stationery heading (note the date!) Colby was one of the first to sell pit dogs to the general public.

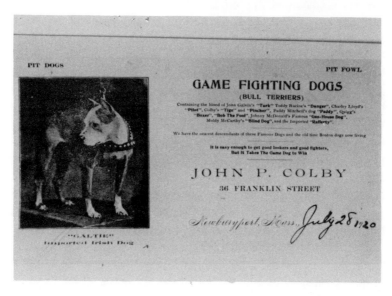

PIT DOGS   PIT FOWL

GAME FIGHTING DOGS
(BULL TERRIERS)

Containing the blood of John Galvin's "Tark" Teddy Racine's "Danger", Charley Lloyd's
"Pilot", Colby's "Tige" and "Pincher", Paddy Mitchell's dog "Paddy", Quigg's
"Boxer", "Bob The Fool", Johnny McDonald's Famous "Gas-House Dog",
Muldy McCarthy's "Blind Dog", and the Imported "Rafferty".

We have the nearest descendants of these Famous Dogs and the old time Boston dogs now living

It is easy enough to get good lookers and good fighters,
But It Takes The Game Dog to Win

JOHN P. COLBY
36 FRANKLIN STREET

Newburyport, Mass. July 28 1920

"GALTIE"
Imported Irish Dog

ly, is way back in the pedigrees of many dogs across the country. Since he is so far back in all those pedigrees, you would not expect him to be still around. But he is still alive, twelve years old and still siring pups. Perhaps, "Grampa" (as Howard calls him) will go on forever—like the Reverend Heinzl himself!

UGLY IS BEAUTIFUL

Richard F. Stratton

(*Pit Bull Gazette,* Fall 1976)

Is the American Pit Bull Terrier ugly? That may not be the burning question of the age, but it is worth considering. Obviously, some people—much to the amazement of the Pit Bull fanciers—do consider the breed to be a trifle homely. As an example, Dr. Leon Whitney, the famous author and veterinarian once mentioned the American Pit Bull Terrier as a breed that he particularly admired, but he allowed that the dogs had a homely and pig-like appearance. He emphasized, however, that appearance was of little consequence and that it was the "cold steel of the mind" that was what really counted.

Actually, as we all know, beauty is in the eye of the beholder. If you are accustomed to Collies with their absurdly narrow heads and long pretty coats (that are forever tangled and knotted), then the Pit Bull with his burly build and "lantern jaw" will probably look a little ominous to you. Actually however, I think Pit Bulls have a tendency to take the prizes in both directions. Some of them have such a bad case of the "uglies" that they are downright laughable! Others have the beauty and grace of a young mountain lion and would be hard to beat (in anyone's eyes) by any other breed. The problem is that *some* of our best dogs may look like mutts that most people wouldn't even bother to pick up off the streets! The same thing is true of other performance breeds. A show Setter, for example, has a ponderous head and an exaggerated coat which, I suppose, is to make him beautiful, while many of the field trial winners are hardly recognizable as a pure breed! Another example is the marvelous Border Collie, who could no more win a dog show than Lassie could herd sheep, but which is to be the most admired, and which has the better breeding?

Above: Deucy, a Lightner female (descended from Spook) that later became the property of Pete Sparks. **Right:** Snoopy, a tough, rugged dog, and very game. Both sides of his pedigree trace directly back to Tudor's Spike. **Below:** Limbeck's Old Gold, a Wallace-bred dog that Limbeck wrote many articles about in the middle fifties.

117

Isn't it possible to have your cake and eat it too? That is, can't we breed for gameness *and* for a good looking dog at the same time? Well, certainly it is possible—if we maintain our priorities. and put gameness first. It sounds simple, but it is much easier said than done. Besides—when a big scruffy looking dog turns out to be an "ace," somehow there is just not a better looking dog around—anywhere!

It is easy to be led astray once we begin selecting primarily on the basis of appearance. I have noted that some individuals have, after hearing about the Old Family Red Nose strain, decided that they want to start a new strain based on the blue nose that is sometimes seen in this breed. The implied assumption here is that the red nose dogs were bred for the color of their nose, but the truth is that they were *not*. It just so happened that a number of dogs from the Old Family (an inbred Irish strain) breedings just happened to throw a lot of red nosed dogs. When these individuals were bred to each other, they produced all red nosed pups. The appeal of these dogs was their *gameness* and *not* the color of their noses. As a matter of fact, most of the early dog men had a hard time getting used to those red noses. In fact, Mr. Lightner, who bred many of the progenitors of what later came to be known as the red nosed dogs dropped that line of dogs, partly because they were running too big for him, but also because he didn't like the red noses.

Well, the truth of the matter is that red nosed dogs look pretty good once you get used to them and are aware of the spectacular gameness that has generally been associated with the strain. For those that don't think so, let's just say that "ugly is beautiful!"

HISTORY ANYONE?

Ralph Greenwood

(*Pit Bull Gazette*, May 1978)

The following account was sent to us by Greg Replogle, a fancier from New Mexico. It is reprinted in part from the 1815 First American Edition of Wood's *Natural History*. Many people believe that the English bull of this period in history was crossed to produce the American Pit Bull Terrier, while others claim that this was the original American Pit Bull Terrier, before they were imported into the United States. I will let you be the judge.

The English Bull Dog

The Bull dog is said, by all who have had an opportunity of judging its capabilities, to be, with the exception of the game cock, the most courageous animal in the world.

Its extraordinary courage is so well known as to have passed into a proverb, and to have so won the admiration of the British nation that we have been pleased to symbolize our peculiar tenacity of purpose under the emblem of this small but most determined animal. In height, the Bull dog is but insignificant, but in strength and courage there is no dog that can match him. There is hardly any breed of sporting dog which does not owe its high courage to an infusion of Bull dog blood; and it is chiefly for this purpose that the pure breed is continued.

We have long ago abolished those combats between the bull and the dog, of which a few "bull-rings" still remaining in the ground are the sole relics. In these contests the dog was trained to fly at the head of the Bull, and to seize him by the muzzle as he stooped his head for the purpose of tossing his antagonists into the air. When he had once made good his hold it was almost impossible for the bull to shake off his pertinacious foe, who clung firmly, and suffered himself to be swung about as the bull might choose.

There seems, indeed, to be no animal which the Bull dog will not attack without the least hesitation. The instinct of fight is strong within him, and manifests itself actively in the countenance and the entire formation of this creature.

It is generally assumed that the Bull dog must be a very dull and brutish animal, because almost every specimen which has come before the notice of the public has held such a character. For this unpleasant disposition, a celebrated writer and zoologist attempts to account by observing that the brain of the Bull dog is smaller in proportion to its body than of any other dog. But Stonehenge well remarks, that although the Bull dog's brain appears to the eye to be very small when compared with the body, the alleged discrepancy is only caused by the deceptive appearance of the skull. It is that the brain appears to be small when compared with the heavy bony processes and ridges that serve to support the muscles of the head and neck, but if the brain be weighed against the remainder of the body, it will be found rather to exceed the average than to be below it.

According to the same writer, the Bull dog is really a sufficiently intelligent animal, and its mental qualities capable of high cultivation.

In all tasks where persevering courage is required, the Bull dog is quietly eminent, and can conquer many a dog in its own peculiar accomplishment. The idea of yielding does not seem to enter his imagination, and he perseveres until he succeeds or falls. One of these animals was lately matched by his owner to swim a race against a large white Newfoundland dog, and won the race by nearly a hundred yards. The owners of the competing dogs threw them out of a boat at a given signal, and then rowed away as fast as they could pull. The two dogs followed the boat at the best of their speed, and the race was finally won by the Bull dog. It is rather remarkable that the Bull dog swam with the whole of his neck out of the water, while the Newfoundland only showed the upper part of his head above the surface.

THE WAY IT WAS

The Farmer

(Pit Bull Gazette, Spring 1977)

Since many people who own Pit Bulls today have never seen a professional contest, it should be stated for their benefit what was perfectly obvious to one who had watched hundreds of money fights; dogs don't all bite the same. Even as the dogs were not equally game, or equally quick, or equally strong, they also did not bite equally hard.

Some Pit Bulls could fight for two hours and never break the skin, although most dogs that made it to the pit for money could do a fair amount of damage. However, some few dogs stood so far above the others in this category, that all dog men who had seen them, friend and foe alike, agreed they were "hard biters".

120

The (English) Bulldog, one of the breeds whose ancestry purportedly entered into the development of the American Pit Bull, but which now diverges radically from the latter in aspects of temperament and physical prowess.

Nothing so moved an old time Pit Bull fancier to eloquence as the memory of a "hard biter". While the deep game dog has been universally sought, the gambler's little darling was the ruthless executioner who could disable his opponent with the first hold he took. Dogs by the names of "Black Jack", "Benny Bob", "Spike", "Jimmy Boots", "Mandigo", and "White Rock" have become legends in various parts of the country. Those dogs, because of their natural ability to bite, were as close to a "sure thing" as a gambler will get.

To the dog fighter, the hard biter offered in addition to the awesome display of brute destructiveness, a cliff-hanging suspense, generated by the fact that very often no one knew how game the dog was. He usually demolished his opponents in his "auditions" and no one ever saw him in trouble. It was usually unspoken, but backer and opponent alike harbored a secret suspicion that he'd turn and run if he had to take what he was dishing out. Some hard biters got the opportunity to prove that they were, indeed, game dogs. Others the reverse. But it rarely happened, because hard biting dogs were rare and they seldom met one another.

Why were they rare? Every dog fighter that ever stepped into a pit dreamed of having one of those crippling, shocking, iron jawed alligators in his hands. Couldn't that trait be consistently

The start of a classic match in the thirties between Corvino's Smilin' Jack and Emerson's Thunder. Both dogs had it all: wrestling ability, hard bite, indestructability, and gameness.

122

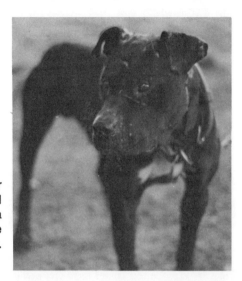

Crenshaw's Hurt, litter brother to Grand Champion Art, and a great hardbiting, game dog in his own right.

reproduced in the breed? Apparently not. I never heard of the sons of "Black Jack" or "Spike" duplicating their sire's abilities although many fine fighting dogs sprang from those lines. Admittedly, there were families of dogs that seemed to be harder biters than others; but I'm not talking about the kind of better than average biter. I'm talking about the dogs that bite an opponent in the chest and kill him if the owner didn't give up the fight. The super biters. *They* were rare.

They will become even more rare . . . for two reasons. (1) They can only be identified under pit conditions. (2) Whatever physiological and conformational traits that play a part in giving the dog his biting advantage are not readily visible to the breeder.

Let's take a look at the first problem . . . identifying the truly hard biter.

Look at "Old Tige" hang on that sack. "Locks them jaws right up, Boy." Well, that sack (or leather strap or piece of rope, or cowhide) doesn't have him by the front leg, jamming him into the corner, trying to tear his shoulder out. You might be surprised to see that "Old Tige" couldn't get his teeth together under such conditions.

Against a worthy opponent, a hard biting dog could take a shoulder hold and immediately penetrate the hide, sink his fangs through an inch and a half of muscle and clamp it like a vice. Muscle was bruised and torn, nerves were cut, the whole area filled with blood and became inoperative in a few minutes. Your average good fighting dog took the same hold, broke the skin, pinched the muscle and bruised it, while the light biter, (who in his own way may have been a fine fighting dog) didn't break the skin, but bruised the muscle. The effect of one was immediate, while the last was scarcely noticeable. These effects were only valid when tested against a comparable athlete.

Many a gambler was dismayed to see that his hard biting champion, that had literally destroyed his no-talent brother at home, couldn't break an egg when confronted by a conditioned pit dog. Why did a dog bite hard against one opponent and not another? Why did he bite hard on a rag, but not in the pit? Well, for one thing, the rag didn't fight back.

Like a puncher, he needed to have his feet on the floor to get power. He needed to set his feet, use his shoulders, back and neck to drive those teeth home. If his opponent could back him up, keep him off balance, take away his leverage, he did a lot to lessen the power of his bite. Consequently most hard biting dogs were also strong dogs. They could take the advantage and keep it. They were conditioned by men who knew what they had and didn't take the bite out of them by conditioning them for a marathon. Since strength was so important, they never really knew until they set him down with another pit quality dog.

By the way, real dog fighters knew this. Anytime you hear of a Pit Bull being "sicced" on a cur dog, or a puppy or whatever, you can bet it's not a dog fighter tuning up his champion, but some nut amateur stroking his ego. Can you imagine A.J. Foyt testing his "Indy" car by blowing off somebody's '57 Chevy?

From there, we go to the second problem of breeding hard biting dogs. What about the physiology and conformation? Look at the pictures of those legendary hard biters. Their heads were all shapes. It didn't seem to matter if the dog had a long muzzle or short; whether he was undershot or had an even bite; whether the head was big or small. Teeth not only frequently did not meet evenly, but were not necessarily long and sharp. Whatever common denominator of bone and muscle relationship that existed in those hard biting dogs is not readily apparent.

I suspect that there is a strong correlation between the length of

Grand Champion Art. This dog was a veritable powerhouse. He blew right through five straight opponents, outclassing them in every way.

the coronoid process on the jaw, and the attachment of the *temporal fossa* muscle. It stands to reason that the farther the *temporal fossa* muscle is attached from the pivot point of the lower jaw, the greater the leverage that can be applied in closing the mouth. If this is true, then brood stock could be selected on the basis of measurements of the bones and muscles of the skull. All it takes is a breeder who can dissect the heads of his broodstock before breeding since this muscle and its attachment are internal!

Seriously, there is a greater pitfall in attempting to breed selectively for a hard bite. Bulldogs are what they are because of their hearts, not their teeth. Whenever a breeder has selected for a physical quality rather than gameness, he has invariably lost the gameness. A bulldog without gameness is like a car without a driver . . . the horse-power's no good until it's driven. Regardless of how hard he *can* bite, he won't bite hard unless he *wants* to.

I remember sitting in one of those smoke filled motel room bull sessions on the eve of a convention and listening to dog men discuss the possibilities of producing hard-biting dogs. The late Frank Fitzwater put an end to the discussion when he said, "Boys, breed your *game* dogs and you'll *get* your fightin' dogs."

125

Apache Rusty Joke, a remnant of the Old Family Red Nose line. He was sired by Wilder's Geronomo II out of Wilder's Flame.

BULLDOGS & DRAGONS

Richard F. Stratton

(Pit Bull Gazette, Summer 1977*)*

More years ago than I care to remember, my second-grade teacher read a story to the class about a dragon that preyed upon a group of gnome-like creatures. Now of course, the dragon was the villain of the book, but a small group of us were iconoclastic enough to side with the dragon. After all, the dragon was a much more exciting creature then the gnomes. He was huge and power-ful, and he could fly and breath fire, too! Besides, we reasoned, it wasn't the dragon's fault that he had to eat gnomes for a living. Well, of course, the dragon was finally destroyed toward the end of the story, and my friends and I observed a suitable period of mourning. Now after forty years, I don't remember the name of the book that was read to us, but I never forgot that dragon!

I don't know if dragons will ever receive redemption, but I know that some of us were ahead of our time in protesting the attempted extermination of such predators as hawks and mountain lions. It is not that any of us enjoy the suffering caused by the predation of the various types of carnivores; it is simply that you don't eliminate suffering by eliminating the predators. With the predators gone, the population is still controlled by disease and starvation. And predators are some of the most interesting animals—not to mention some of the most magnificent! A predator is likely to be a more intelligent animal too, as it requires more versatility to catch and eat animals than to eat grass or leaves. Those of us who are able to appreciate the songbird and the hawk, the ant and the ant lion, and yes, even the host and the parasite, are those who have come to know nature as she really is, rather than as some idealistic dreamer might prefer. Many of the modern "nature freaks" are in love with a dream of their own making that has little relationship to the real world.

Georgia holding Squeeze.

Left: Louis Sylvestri with Jiggs (taken in 1950). **Right:** Fulkerson's Little Maggie, a daughter of Lightner's Spook.

The point of all this is that the world is not always as its seems. In fact, if we look a little more deeply into certain situations, we find that things are sometimes nearly opposite of how they first appeared. Perhaps the following will help to illustrate the point. A few years ago there appeared on television a dog story that contained a Pit Bull as the villain. Near the beginning of the story, our hero (an otterhound) is jumped upon and soundly trounced by the Pit Bull. Just to make sure we know that the Pit Bull is a villain, several characters of the story (mainly hound men) make very disparaging comments about the worthlessness of the breed and how it was a bully and bred "solely for scrapping" and was good for nothing else. Now if our screen writers had known what they were doing they would have had their character simply admonish the Pit Bull's owner for allowing him to run loose, rather than to talk the foolishness that they did.

Obviously, the Pit Bull is good for something besides fighting. His worth as a catch dog is well established. He has long been used as a hunting dog, mainly for wild boar but also as a "still trailer" for raccoon. On top of that, nearly all Pit Bulls make excellent pets and house guards. Their nature with people is much better than that of most breeds.

128

Above: Don Livingston's dog Spike begins his job of rounding up a stray pig and getting it back in its pen. **Below:** This picture provides the reader with a comparison in size and demonstrates the incredible power and skill that must be possessed by the Pit Bulldog in order to perform as a catch dog.

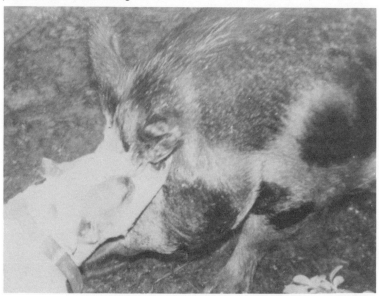

Left: Ed Weldon's young dog Sugarfoot with a badger that he killed on a hunting foray with his owners.
Below: Two Lightner dogs kick up the dust as they wrestle for holds in a roll many decades ago. Serious pit dog men today don't school their dogs outside a pit in the dirt.

As for the charge of being a bully, it all depends on your point of view. To the hounds the Pit Bull may seem like a bully, even though he is invariably smaller than the hound, but the object of the hounds affection is the raccoon, an animal considerably smaller than the hounds, and to top it off, he rarely gets to go "one-on-one" with a hound. Rather, he has to handle several at one time! Now, what was that breed again that was called a bully?

CLOSE ENCOUNTERS OF THE CUR KIND

Richard Stratton

(Pit Bull Gazette, November 1978)

First, let me reassure all of my friends that this article is not about their breeding programs! (And is not about mine either). Rather, this will be a series of articles that will appear at irregular intervals and will deal with incidents in which a particular Pit Bull has been in a fight with a non Pit Bull. In telling these stories, it is not my intention to encourage anyone to allow his Pit Bull to fight a cur. The contrary, in fact, for such fights are a cruel thing. Although the cur may be full of fight in the beginning, he soon becomes a beaten and terrorized animal. Unfortunately, the Pit Bull is unable to comprehend that another animal would not delight in fighting (just as he does), so he won't let go—no matter how much his opponent yells!

I have often been amazed by the number of people that seem to find nothing wrong with a cur "taking his lumps." A breeder of Staffordshires took great delight in telling my wife and me about how his show champion killed his neighbor's Husky. The thing that dismayed us the most was that it took twelve minutes for the "kill", and our Staff enthusiast watched the whole thing from his kitchen window and made no effort to stop it. (This incidentally was a man that was fanatically opposed to pit fighting!)

There may be times, though, when a cur deserves to take a few lumps. A case in point was a time that I unleashed my dog Honeybear on a Great Dane. The justification in this circumstance was that the Great Dane was mauling a nine-year-old boy. I was perhaps a hundred yards away, and I was the closest person to the scene. As I ran through the heavy snow to save the

Greenwood's Champion Freddie

boy, I finally remembered that I had a veritable "anti-missile missile" on a leash who could not only get to the rescue more quickly than I, but would handle things more expeditiously once there! So I dropped Honeybear's leash, and he sped unerringly toward the giant dog. The Dane was shaking the frightened boy by the shoulder when a 45-pound tornado came streaking at him out of nowhere, knocking him loose from the helpless boy, and the two rolled in the snow. Quick as a cat, Honeybear downed the gigantic dog and shook him until he rattled. The Dane howled in pain and finally tore loose and bolted away. I grabbed Honeybear up quickly before he could give chase.

The other people, by this time, had arrived at the scene. They were full of praise even suggested nominating a dog hero award for him. I directed their attention to the injured boy and suggested that someone find the Dane and his owner; otherwise the boy would have to undergo the painful rabies treatment. Then I spirited Honeybear away. It had suddenly occurred to me that I was technically in violation of the felony dog-fighting bill that the "loonies" had recently rammed through the state assembly!

132

STYLES & WILES
Richard F. Stratton
(Pit Bull Gazette, May 1978)

What is the best style of fighting for a dog is a question that was often debated and discussed by the old time pit dog men. If we examine the opinions of a large number of old timers, we find a certain consensus of thought. Generally speaking, a dog that fought the head was preferred, and other things being equal, the leg dog was not in high favor because he left himself open to having his nose chewed on. (The nose is a very vulnerable spot on a dog.) Note the key phrase "other things being equal." It is an important qualifier, and perhaps a few stories about particular dogs with specific fighting skills will illustrate the point.

Let's start with "Searcy Jeff," as he was always a good demonstrator of why a dog should not be a leg dog. "Jeff" was a brindle

Dolye Reddick's Champion Buster, by Boze out of Glory Bee.

Left: Mike Kerns and Red. Red was the dog that could break legs like matchsticks! **Below:** Wallace's Jeff, son of King Cotton. This dog was loaned to Howard Hadley in the fifties to help improve the bloodlines of the Staffordshire Terrier.

dog with yellow eyes (his sire was an Old Family Red Nose dog), and he was a little shy with people. However, he would kill your dogs for you just as fast as you wanted to set them down for him. "Jeff" was all but unscarred except for his right front leg. For he would practically place that leg in the other dog's mouth. As soon as a dog was "suckered" into taking that leg, "Jeff" had him by the nose, and that, my friend, was the beginning of the end. For "Jeff" had such devastating biting power that he could literally destroy a dog in short order with a nose or head hold.

On the other hand, there was Kern's "Red", a dog that always went right for a front leg. In his case, however, things went differently. Once "Red" got the leg, he shook out the hold so hard and fast that everything was a blur. Not only was the other dog unable to get "Red" by the nose but, as often as not, he was actually lifted clear of the ground by the violence of "Red's" shaking power. Although, it was rare for a dog to be able to break another dog's leg—especially a bulldog's—"Red" broke his opponents' legs with grim regularity, and his matches didn't last long. Who would win if we could magically match "Searcy Jeff" and "Red?" What wins when an irresistible force meets an immovable object?

Then there was "Dillinger" (also known as Corvino's "Braddock") who was not a particularly hard-biting dog, but he had a way of always getting a dog's ear and letting him wear himself out trying to get to him. The old, boring-in type chest dogs were cannon fodder for him. The harder they drove the more quickly they tired themselves out, as "Braddock" led them around by the ear. So successful was "Braddock" that he even won a match when he was twelve years old and was reported to have had fourteen wins. On the other hand, the immortal "White Rock", who was nearly always listed in the top three of all time great dogs, was a chest dog that nobody could hold out. Ear dogs were as much cannon fodder for him as chest dogs were for "Braddock", for he merely pushed them up against the pit wall and bored right into the chest and let the other dog hold that ear . . . if he could. Again, who would win if we could magically level the weights and neutralize the time spread? That's a question for which no one has the answer, but I think most old timers would give the edge to "White Rock."

In any case, you're beginning to get the idea of compensating factors. All the dogs mentioned had all the normal advantages in

Above: Farrell's Red Buck, one of the original Old Family Red Nose dogs.
Below: G.W. Hubbard with Braddock, the dog with 14 wins and who defeated hard-biting dogs by outfinessing them.

Wallace's Brindle
Tiger. One of the
typical old-time
Wallace dogs.

addition to a specific super-normal ability. But there were other dogs who won like clock-work even though there was not an outstanding trait—at least, not an obvious one. These were dogs that seemingly couldn't be hurt. They absorbed punishment like a sponge, then got up off the pit floor to win. Old Armitage's "Cue" was an example of that type of dog, and it was often the preferred type of many old timers.

Getting down into the realm of the normal-but-tricky bulldogs, we have Wallace's "Red Rube". As Wallace said, the only danger of death to his opponents was a rather remote chance of a heart attack or perhaps being struck by a lightning bolt; yet he won some matches and stopped a host of dogs. Where did he fight? Would you believe a pinch of skin underneath the lower jaw? But he was there 90% of the time and whenever a dog tried to twist away, "Rube" went right with him, just as relaxed as could be, completely frustrating his opponent.

As we can see, the question of what style is best is not so simple as it first appeared. Also, we have insight into why it was so difficult for an old timer to name the "most outstanding dog he had ever seen."

Lou Diehl and his wife strike an old-fashioned pose with their dog Grip for a Christmas card.

THE FOUNDATION
Richard Stratton

(Pit Bull Gazette, February 1978)

While, much to my satisfaction, my book on the American Pit Bull Terrier was received with enthusiastic and nearly unanimous approval, *some* of the American Staffordshire Terrier people did not care for the book at all. My major crime, it seems, was saying that the Staff and the Pit Bull should no longer be considered the same breed. Now I must admit that I am a little surprised at all this unhappiness about this particular point, since for years Staf people have beat their breast and moaned about how difficult it was to escape the "Pit Bull image"! The fact that the Staf people were the ones unhappy about the separate-breed thesis and that most Pit Bull people applauded the idea says something about the "image" of the two breeds.

Now we must remember, of course, that the Staf started out as a Pit Bull over forty years ago when it was recognized by the American Kennel Club with aid and encouragement of the Colbys and other influential Pit Bull people, as well as that of show dog people. It is only natural to wonder what went wrong, for the Staf has never attained the popularity with the public that the Pit Bull has, and, of course, most Pit Dog men regard the breed with very little respect.

I think the main problem was the Staf breeders became slavishly devoted to show points and were never concerned with gameness or performance in any way. Of course, many of the people were against the fighting of dogs. But that is true of most Pit Bull people too, but they breed to stud dogs, at least, that are proven game—at least the good breeders do! Staf people seemed to feel that they could just take gameness for granted. In fact, many years ago a famous Staf breeder made a pronouncement that breeding for show was a much greater challenge than breeding for the pit because when you bred for the pit you were breeding for only one trait (gameness), but when you bred for show you were breeding for a variety of things (show points). He went on to say that some pit dog men bred their dogs so game that you had to feed them with a shovel. Well, on the second point, our Staf man has confus-

An example of the American Staffordshire Terrier, sometimes called the "Am Staf."

139

Jim Marshall's
Deacon, by Allen's
Tudor Red and out of
Marshall's Lady Judy.

ed aggressiveness with gameness. Very few pit dog men will tolerate a "man-fighter" anyway, mainly because most "man-fighters"
turn out to be "curs". Even aggressiveness toward other dogs is
not a reliable indicator of gameness. Some of the gamest dogs have
been easy-going animals that showed little aggressiveness outside
the pit. In the first point, our Staf expert simply reveals inordinate
ignorance. Gameness is a simple name for a complex trait that probably involves blood chemistry, heart and lung structure, brain
chemistry, neurological structures, and tissue structure, among
other things. There is probably at least one gene for each of these
traits and very likely even more. The poly-genetic nature of
gameness makes it a trait that is indeed a challenge to breed for. In
any case, Staf people, including our "expert" have certainly failed
miserably to maintain gameness—as easy as that task should have
been! Ah well, none of this means we shouldn't show our dogs, of
course. But, we should remember our priorities—gameness first.
In fact, gameness must be a starting point, the foundation on
which all else is built. Luckily, with the ADBA, we have a better
standard than the Staf people. In fact, it is one of the best of all
show standards, and, obviously, considerable thought and study
went into it. But let us not be blinded by it! There are, and there
will continue to be, dogs that don't fit the standard but leave

140

nothing to be desired in wrestling ability, or anything else! Good dogs come in all manner of shapes and builds, and I know our editor will agree with me on this. So let us show our dogs for the fun of it, so the public may see what a Pit Bull "is really like". But neither let us forget that it is not what a Pit Bull looks like that makes him the greatest fighting machine the world has ever known.

THE WAY IT WAS

The Farmer

(*Pit Bull Gazette,* February 1978)

"Gamest dog that ever looked through a collar," . . . "Front running cur," . . . "Dead game" . . . "Couldn't take what he handed out." How many times have you heard Bulldog people use those terms? Especially those who go back to the days when dogs were commonly fought in the pit? And isn't it the truth that one man's "dead game" was another man's "cur"?

"Game" and "Cur" have dominated the conversation of American Pit Bull fanciers since the breed began, because it is a natural fact that without gameness, you don't have a fighting dog.

Pat Carver's Baby Jane.

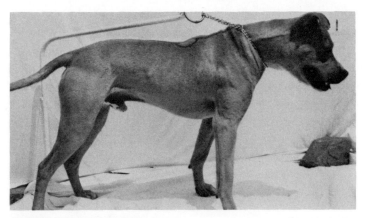

Above: Newton's Pistol, Jr. won a long tough match. He is by Offer's Pistol and out of Reuver's Biddy. **Below:** Bert Sorrells and Goober, a great Bulldog.

Paul Johnson and his five-
time winner Grand Champion
Sinful Sailor.

Most people who are fanciers of any breed of dog are fascinated
by what Bulldog people call "gameness". Many's the time I've
been to a dog show and listened to owners of everything from Irish
Wolfhounds to Lhasa Apsos talk about their particular favorite's
"courage", "loyalty", "persistence" etc. Those are just other
words for what *we* refer to as gameness. It's pretty hard to lie
about a shallow rib cage, straight stifle or other conformation
points, because they're right out there for all to see. But talk about
courage, and man, watch the imaginations go wild. Every
handler's dog has a heart like a lion.

That's not a problem as long as there's no way to find out, but
the Pit Bull fancier was frequently faced with a "Put-up-or-shut-
up" situation. For that reason we have become much more defini-
tive about those general terms used to describe gameness in other
breeds; and also more polarized in our opinions. Many a valued
friendship has been destroyed by the injudicious use of the word
"game" and "cur".

So when is a dog "game" and when is he a "cur"? And what distinguished him from "dead game" and "rank cur"?

If we use the commonly held opinion that a game dog was a dog
that wouldn't quit and a cur was one that would quit we're going
to be in trouble, because it was the contention of some of the most
successful dog fighters and breeders of the past that "they'll all
quit". True, some of them took their death and didn't quit, but

143

that doesn't mean they couldn't have quit under different conditions.

In a previous column we discussed gameness and defined it as the "will to win". If we can accept that definition, we can also accept that anything that has to do with "will" is relative to other values that also have a "will": For example, the will to survive.

As soon as we inject the possibility of relative values into the discussion, we take a giant step toward understanding the driving force that makes the ideal of the American Pit Bull Terrier different from the ideal of all other breeds. We ask him to have the will to win (or dominate) that is greater than his will to survive. If we had the opportunity to watch hundreds of dogs in pit contests (as many old-timers did), we would realize that there are two huge variables in these two competing value systems.

(1) That the will to dominate varies within the individual. For example, some bitches did not fight the same when they were in heat. Some males dogs did not fight bitches as hard as other males. A sick or undernourished dog would not be as game as when healthy. The list could be much longer.

(2) That the threat to survival varies with the opponent, conditions of the contest, and the dog's assessment of the threat at the time.

I believe that a Bulldog somehow equates his ability to dominate his opponent with his ability to survive. You very rarely saw a dog quit if he dominated the fight completely, even if he was very badly injured. However, when he lost the initiative, started to go down, was unable to take his favorite holds, his will to dominate began to be tested. For that reason, dogs that fought the ear or the nose were enormously successful even if they couldn't bite hard because they frustrated their opponent by holding him off and were able to dominate the action even if they weren't punishing.

It also seems obvious that when a dog becomes fatigued, he will be less able to dominate a fresher opponent, and as fatigue becomes severe, he will recognize some threat to his survival which will be computed against how badly he wants to win. There have been many cases where both dogs were going into fatigue-induced shock, but one dog quit before the other. Obviously, some combination of factors gave one dog's will to win precedence over the other dog's will to survive.

Andre Giroux's Paddy, a two-time winner and a son of the fabulous Boomerang. He is running a slat-type mill.

When a well-conditioned pit dog goes into shock and stands in his corner, does that make him a cur? I don't think so; just not "dead game".

On the other hand, if Bowser screams, turns and jumps the pit the first time he goes down, I would say he's gone a long way in the direction of being labeled a cur. Somewhere within these two extremes lay the vast majority of the ancestors of our present-day American Pit Bull Terriers. Hopefully, the dogs on our pedigrees represent the higher end of the scale.

How did the really successful dog-fighters select their prospects? Many a conversation between Bulldog men reflected the importance of selection. For example, one well known fancier frequently says, "A match well made is a match half won." Another time a beginning dog-fighter asked a more experienced man (who should have known because he lost more than he won), "what is the most common mistake made in conditioning?" The response was . . . "Conditioning the wrong dog." So how do you determine how game a dog is? (note that we are not asking if he is game or not game.)

The opinion of some present-day breeders notwithstanding, I submit that you can't tell by the look in his eye. You have to bring

145

The white-headed dog parries a lightning grab for a leg by pulling it back and putting pressure on the head of the red dog. Again, this was a roll that took place many years ago.

into play the conflicting forces of the will to survive and the will to dominate. You have to "roll" them to see what you've got. Serious practioners of the sport (that is, those who put their money on the line) rolled their young dog for three reasons; to school the dog, to determine the dog's ability, and to determine the dog's degree of gameness. I never knew a serious dog man who rolled his dogs for *any other reason.* Sadism is a waste of time, a waste of valuable animals and is an abuse of the purpose for which the dog has been bred. Sadists have been scorned and ridiculed by serious fanciers and should continue to be ostracized with every means at our disposal. However, if the dogs had not been rolled and fought, there wouldn't be an American Pit Bull Terrier today.

How did the dedicated fancier conduct his rolls? Obviously in looking for gameness, he tried to simulate pit conditions that induced a dog to quit. The degree to which the dog resisted the temptation to save his hide had a lot to do with deciding whether he could win. We already have recognized that fatigue and dominance are the major factors that influence the will to win. (Pain probably enters into it but I believe a Bulldog's threshold of resistance to pain is so high in the heat of battle, that it's not significant.) To insure that some semi-balance of the fatigue would be felt without burning the dog up, dogs were usually rolled when they were a little fat. Thus, they didn't have to stand and watch them for two hours. The dog they wanted to know about was usually rolled with a bigger opponent. The smaller dog would tire

146

more quickly from pushing the heavier weight and would also have considerably less ability to dominate a bigger, stronger opponent. The idea was to attempt to discourage your prospect as quickly as possible (after, of course, he had developed his confidence in schooling rolls) and make your judgment of whether to match him or not without leaving his best fight in the gym.

It was a truism that the more a man knew about fighting dogs, the less he needed to roll them. His experience (and lack of subjective involvement) led him to rely on signs. These signs were never absolute, but were very subtle and were widely open to interpretation. Thus when a successful dog-fighter brought a dog to the Pit and said laconically that the dog, "had never made a bad sign", he spoke volumes with that phrase; much more than some beginner who bought the dog because he was the color of his wife's hair.

The surest "sign" is to look for a holding dog. A dog that takes his hold and keeps it. Old timers liked a dog that would only swap one hold for a better one. Beware the dog who had a good hold on the nose, ear, or chest and when he went down, released it to grasp frantically for everything in sight. A game dog would keep his good hold and try to wrestle his way up with it. A really game dog would work the hold from the bottom and not put any great priority in being on top. He might also get killed doing this.

The more game the fighter, the more pressure he would put on his opponent. Even if he could not get a good hold, he'd always have a nip somewhere, trying to get a better one. Many dogs that were not so game would keep a good hold if they were up, but never kept a hold when they were down. They could win a fight against a dog they could outwrestle but look out when they got tired and started to go down.

Of course a "turn" was always a telltale sign. If a dog turned his head and shoulders away from the other dog, it was a sure sign he was thinking about getting out. If he fuzzed up at the base of the tail when he lost the advantage, or if he howled and cried when bit, chances were that he was not a pit prospect. These were not the only signs. Dogs were judged and evaluated for gameness by the way they scratched, the way they looked at their opponent (or more important, if they looked *away* from their opponent) and how they felt in the corner.

147

Above: The match between Smilin' Jack and Thunder continues. Note that coat and tie were worn to these events in the thirties! Today, a carpet would probably be used in place of the canvas tarp pictured. **Below:** Smilin' Jack gets Thunder up against the pit wall and, for the time being, has him nearly helpless.

Occasionally, you would hear someone brag about his dog's gameness by saying he had been "two dogged". In other words, a fresh dog had been put on him after he had gone long enough to stop his first opponent. The only thing that tells is that the handler couldn't see what he should have seen with one opponent. It meant nothing as a qualititive assessment. The first, and for that matter the second, dog could have been a totally inept bum and you simply were looking at the best of three bums; or they could have indeed been long, hard rolls and your game dog had left 20% of his ability behind him. It was the task of the handler to select the opponents in the roll to make the best possible judgment with the least possible trauma.

In an attempt to put a handle on this very nebulous subject, I think we can state with assurance that the best dog men couldn't tell much about a dog's gameness in less than 20 minutes. They might roll him for less time and decide to match him based on his *ability*, but they were *betting* on his gameness.

For in the final analysis, the test was going to the pit for money; one man's conditioning, breeding and judgment against the other man's. When the men who created this breed looked at a dog, they didn't ask, "Is he game or cur?", they asked, "Is he game enough to win?"

SUPER DOG OR STUPID DOG?

Richard F. Stratton

(*Bloodlines Journal*, January-February 1976)

Those of us who are involved with the American (Pit) Bull Terrier are inclined to regard the breed as a super dog—and with good reason! The A.P.B.T. is possessor of great strength, courage, and agility, and is capable of truly amazing feats. However, some of the gentry that do not really know our breed but feel compelled to discredit it have come up with another "twist." First, they tried to say the breed was vicious, but this fiction has been largely discredited now. So now the word is being put out that the A.P.B.T. is not too bright. What a way to add insult to injury! When I hear of such stories, I am reminded of Albert Payson Terhune's response to reports that the Collie was a treacherous breed. In essence, he said that that particular idea was first expressed when the Fool Killer was away on vacation.

Now, I am not here to say that our breed is absolutely the smartest dog that exists. I once decided to try to find out just what was the smartest breed of dog. I decided to look first at breeds of dogs whose work would seem to place an emphasis on intelligence. I studied, to some degree, Border Collies, Queensland Heelers, Kelpies, bird dogs, and retrievers. All of these dogs are extremely tractable, but even the partisans of these breeds are seldom wont to claim that their dogs are the most intelligent. The dogs simply have an inborn urge of some kind. For example, a Border Collie has the desire to "stalk" sheep. All of this pap about a sheepdog loving the sheep and wanting to care for them is sheer nonsense! However, the Border Collie *is* gentle with stock and has the urge to "gather" sheep. So strong is his urge that he must be chained up at night or he will herd the sheep all night long! However, evidence that the "herding" urge is an embellishment of the stalking

Sarona Dinah-mite, another modern remnant of the Old Family Red Nose strain.

Ted Jessop with Green-
wood's Mountain Boy.

instinct is the fact that nearly all young untrained Border Collies or Kelpies want to bite the sheep. As for bird dogs, they simply are fascinated by birds in the same way that sheep dogs are by sheep. In fact, the "point" of the bird dog is very similar to the "eyeing" of stock by a sheep dog. As for retrievers, well, they simply have been bred to be tractable, "birdy", and to want to retrieve objects that fall from the air. I was amused the other day while out playing tennis. One of my famous, if errant, overhand smashes had somehow gone clear out of the court and over the fence! However, I had seen a boy out walking his Labrador Retriever, and I knew we would soon have our ball back. There was just no way that Lab could resist his urge to retrieve!

Another group of dogs that appears to be especially intelligent are the "toys" or "lap dogs." These dogs do seem to be especially alert and responsive. Obviously, these little dogs have been selectively bred for centuries for their charm. However, small Pit Bulls often show the same traits! So obviously size alone has a lot to do with the behavior and appeal of small dogs. Poodles are often touted as the smartest of all dogs, and their excellent record in obedience trials is often given as evidence to this claim. However, if adjustments are made in terms of numbers, we find the Shetland Sheepdog has an even better record! And most experts of this breed indicate that it is the Sheltie's *willingness* to *work* more than intelligence that makes him excel in this field. Incidentally, if the percentage factor is once again taken into account the record of the

151

American Staffordshire Terrier (the show counterpart to the A.P.B.T.) is one of the better ones, too!

Now, I said I wouldn't make any claims for our dog being the smartest breed—and with good reason. Certain tests done by cy – nologists indicate that no one breed of dog has cornered the market in the brains category. But there is no denying that we certainly have our fair share of smart dogs. I am reminded of the Pit Bull that always took his chain in his mouth when he went into his dog house. It seems that there was a large nail in his dog house (left by a careless owner) that the chain used to get caught on. Now, there is "problem solving" that would impress even a cyonologist!

I am also reminded of Pete the Pup, the movie star of the thirties and forties. (Actually, despite word to the contrary, there were several "Pete the Pups" and the circle around the eye *was* painted on.) And, even more, I am reminded of Porky, a Pit Bull that actually talked. She said words like "Mama", "Papa," "Bye-Bye", and (most clearly of all) "eat"! A speech therapy professor from a local university taped Porky's "ravings", and got down on his hands and knees and tried to see how Porky articulated the words. And Bob and Marcella Wise once told me (in confidence) that their house dog, Sister Sue, was able to articulate certain words. (Sorry to let your "secret" out, Bob, but these people need to know who's going to answer the phone if they call your house!)

Well, all kidding aside, the good old Pit Bull may not be faster than a speeding bullet or even able to leap tall buildings in a single bound, but he is truly a super dog of sorts. As for his being stupid, that idea will soon go the same route as the old stereotype of the "dumb athlete." Given time, ridiculous notions will fall of their own weight!

AND A "FILIAL DEGENERATION" TO YOU TOO!

Richard F. Stratton

(Pit Bull Gazette, Fall 1976)

One of the historical breeders who has always been of particular interest to me was D.A. McClintock of Oklahoma. As far as I have been able to ascertain, McClintock never matched a dog; yet, his accomplishments as a breeder were extraordinary, and his line of

Right: Fulkerson's Norma, a daughter of Lightner's Spook (later known as Fulkerson's Spook). **Below:** Sinful (of Sequan Kennels) undergoes the attack phase training in preparation for Schutzhund trials.

Hart's Red Ace, bred by W.C. Roper in the early 50's, won many matches and appears in the pedigree of many modern dogs.

dogs was in particular demand by the dog men of his day. He wrote a number of articles for his contemporary dog magazines, and they make fascinating and instructive reading even today. For example, in one article Mr. McClintock begins by apologizing for a lack of formal education, then goes on to explain filial degeneration, a concept that even bedevils geneticists!

Filial degeneration refers to the tendency of the offspring of any breeding stock to revert to the average of the race or strain. Thus, if the two top dogs in the country are bred together, their offspring have only a remote chance of being as good as either parent. Similarly, in humans, if two geniuses marry and have children, the chances of their producing another genius are also remote. The genes are jumbled, and the tendency is to revert back toward the average. Filial degeneration has often been called the "drag of the race"; however, the same process also works the other way. If two morons marry and have children, chances are their offspring will not be like them. Also, if we breed two "curs" of a good strain together, we have a chance of getting some game pups. There have been some "aces" that came from such breedings. Tudor's "Black Demon" is just one such example. (Now, that does *not* mean that it is all right to breed curs! Please read on before jumping to that conclusion!)

Dog men have often been perplexed by the fact that certain outstanding dogs would not produce when used at stud. The reason, very likely, was that the dogs were not representative of their ancestry. (They were like a good-looking girl springing from

154

Right: Joe Jurgens with Jurgen's Captain Flint in a picture taken in 1919. **Below:** A very old picture of Kelly with Kelly's Peggy. Note how little the Pit Bull has changed throughout the years.

a long line of homely ancestors. The girl may be good-looking herself, but her progeny will likely revert back to the average of her "line"!) That is why it is so important to study the pedigree of the animals we are breeding. Just because a dog is good himself does not mean that he will produce good pups. While it is true that some Pit Bulls who are not game themselves are good producers, I agree with Pat Patrick that this little fact has all-too-often been used as an excuse for breeding to a cur. Whenever we breed to a cur, we are throwing the "wrong" genes back into the hopper to be once again jumbled, and while we may get good results in the first generation, eventually there will be the devil to pay!

Anyway, the question is how do we get around this filial degeneration which looms as such a great obstacle to what we are trying to accomplish. Well, the answer is to breed to a quality line and to work to raise the average of the line. That means *never* breeding to curs and *always* using quality individuals. Yes, I know that means extensive use of inbreeding, and inbreeding is a big bugaboo to many individuals. However, modern geneticists have dispelled many of the old wives' tales about inbreeding, and we need not worry about using it to our heart's content—as long as we are careful to cull out the undesirable traits! It is generally believed that inbreeding causes a decrease in fertility and size; however, hardnosed selectivity can nullify even these effects. Hybrid vigor is a famous phenomenon that is characterized by increased size and vigor in the offspring. However, geneticists have demonstrated highly inbred lines in which the selectivity of stock had been so stringent that the lines actually *lost* vigor when crossed with any other!

Now, gameness very likely consists of a number of different genes that work together to produce the trait. Unfortunately, there are probably a number of genes that nullify or modify the effect of the desired genes. (That's the way things usually work genetically, but of course, no *real* research has been done on gameness!) So our main task in breeding is to purify our strain of these unwanted genes. This takes many generations, and all our work is un-done when some yahoo breeds to a dog whose gameness is suspect. We also always take a chance when we outcross to another strain because we may be throwing into the hopper some of the genes that will modify the effect of the pattern of genes that produces gameness in our stock. However, in my opinion, it is better to breed "best to best" than to stay within a strain but not be sufficiently selective. To sum up;

(1.) Genetics is nearly pure statistics, predictable in only large numbers. Breeding dogs is like rolling dice in that we are jumbling the genes and seeing how they come out on each "throw". *We gain an edge by limiting the possible combinations.*

(2.) Inbreeding enables us to overcome the effect of filial degeneration by *reducing the variety of genes so that we have a better chance of matching desirable genes.*

(3.) Breeding "best to best" is difficult to fault; however, if this is done without regard to strain, results will be less consistent. A greater strain gives us greater uniformity.

(4.) The emphasis should always be on the quality, regardless of the breeding model you use (for example: best to best, inbreeding, outbreeding or whatever). *Selectivity is the single most important factor in breeding.*

BULLDOG TRIUMPHS

Richard F. Stratton

(Pit Bull Gazette, February 1979)

After years of being either vilified or ignored, the good old American Pit Bull Terrier seems to be crashing through all barriers of intolerance and ignorance to capture the general public's admiration. For, given the chance to know him firsthand, the average person seems compelled to grant the Pit Bull, at the very least, a grudging respect. The so-called "outlaw breed" obviously is his own best public relations representative. As evidence of this phenomenon, let me cite a few examples.

Item one involves my own well-publicized trial. I will have much more to say about this in later issues, but for now just let me say that a second trial, lasting four weeks, resulted in a quick "not guilty" verdict. My attorney, flushed with victory after hearing the verdict, informed the judge that the jury was welcome to keep copies of my book that had been entered into evidence, whereupon the jurors announced that they wanted their copies autographed! As I autographed the books, various different members of the jury

Above: A Tosa, the Japanese fighting dog which can weigh up to a hundred and fifty pounds. Surprisingly, a good Pit Bulldog can whip one of these monsters—even going by Japanese rules! **Below:** George Gillman's famous Plumber dog, a litter-mate to Champion Cle.

Sorrell's Bull, a son of Zeke and a producer of quality dogs.

told me how they had nearly all decided they would like to have a Pit Bull! Now, of course, both of my attorneys had indicated previously that they themselves wanted a Pit Bull, but I just wonder if the prosecutor didn't secretly covet one, too! (Incidentally, the attack on the constitutionality of the moronic California law will go on. Contributions were not used for my personal legal fees but are being placed in trust for fighting the law itself. The response, incidentally, was heartwarming, and I thank you all!)

Item two. A recent article in a Japanese newspaper begins (in translation): "I have always believed that the Tosa was the greatest fighting machine of the canine race. But, my friends, I was wrong! A little-known breed in the United States reigns supreme." At this point, I should explain to the readers that dog-fighting is legal in Japan and was once conducted with Akitas, too, but they were not sufficiently competitive with the Tosa. (The Akita is a large long-haired breed and the Tosa looks something like a gigantic heavy-jowled Pit Bull.) The journalist in the Japanese newspaper went on to explain how four American Pit Bull Terriers had been matched against Tosas, and all four won. What particularly impressed the journalist was the fact that one of the Tosas weighed 130 pounds and was a grand champion. His Pit Bull opponent was less than half his size. After taking the bottom for the first twelve minutes, the bulldog got his opponent down and never let him up again! No wonder our journalist was impressed. Even I would

One of the all-time great dogs and producers, Randy Fox's Alvin.

Below: An American Staffordshire Terrier in show stance.

Sequan Mike, the dog with the heart problem.

have doubted that the A.P.B.T. fighting by Japanese rules could defeat the Tosa. (I am indebted to Gil Garcia, incidentally, who brought the paper back from Japan.)

Item three. Frank Ambrose sent me a Xerox copy of a newspaper article headlined "Power-Packed Pit Bull Is Threat To Thugs"! The article tells about a wealthy and vastly experienced attack dog trainer who has decided that the Pit Bull is the world's best candidate as a protection dog. He cites the dog's formidability, good disposition, and small convenient size ("fits nicely into compact cars"). Now here is a man that has had experience with all manner of dogs. While Plunkett (the trainer) is candid about the Pit Bull's formidability ("They can whip any dog in the world."), he is even more impressed by another aspect of the breed: "It's their intelligence. If I can get ten German Shepherds, only three or four may be really bright and easy-to-teach. With Dobermans, it's an even smaller percentage. But with the Pit Bulls, I've never had one that wasn't easy to teach and eager to learn. They are exceptional students."

It is refreshing change, of course, to have favorable coverage for our breed. But don't worry, there will still be an onslaught of the other kind. Even now, I can envision the hack writers and purveyors of hatred polishing their little axes for a "hatchet job" on one of the most remarkable animals that has ever walked the face of the earth.

VENDETTA
Richard F. Stratton
(Pit Bull Gazette, May 1979)

In the last issue of PIT BULL GAZETTE I reported on a newspaper article that was very complimentary of every aspect of the American Pit Bull Terrier. While it was a refreshing change, I predicted that the hate mongers would soon be back peddling their usual drivel. Perhaps "hate mongers" was too all-inclusive a term. Actually, most of the writing is done by reporters whose job it is to write articles that sell newpapers. For that reason, most journalists have a tendency to sensationalize whatever they are reporting. Then, too, we have to take into account that the reporters are

Above: Joan Gilman and John Landry with Landry's Fat Albert.
Below: Jacoby and Lemon's Champion Glover.

Isaacs' Dirty Sally

Dickie Freeman with Cyclone, better known as Honeybear.

Hammonds' Bruno and Katy-Ann with her first litter of pups which includes Macho, Cook's Bad News, and Elliott's Tiger.

spoon-fed a lot of misinformation by supposed experts. And these "experts" are quoted saying incredible nonsense! Obviously, the Pit Bull makes for good copy, especially for the sensationalist-type periodicals, as articles about them have been as numerous as they have been inaccurate. Rather than trying to answer a myriad of writings that have appeared in various newspapers and magazines across the country, let me as an official "expert" (court certified!) state a few basic facts.

Fact one: The American Pit Bull Terrier is a very gentle breed with people. He is highly intelligent, and he has unusual abilities that make him useful to mankind in a variety of ways (*i.e.*, as a catch dog, a hunter, and a reliable personal guard dog, to name just a few). These traits of the breed are a direct result of his ancestors being tried in the pit. The intelligent, tough, and formidable dogs prevailed. Of course, these dogs also had to be game.

And there is evidence that gameness is somehow connected genetically to a steady disposition.

Fact two: The idea of dogfighting being cruel is an absolute myth! If the dogs love what they do, where is the cruelty? Now, of course, the uninformed person has a difficult time comprehending this simple fact. It seems self-evident to them that dogfighting *must* be cruel. But then it once seemed self-evident that the earth was flat. And having virtually the entire world population believing the earth was flat did not succeed in unrounding it one whit! One reason many people can't accept the non-cruelty thesis is that they project their own feelings into the dogs and therefore they can't conceive of an animal that actually enjoys fighting contact. But the Pit Bull does! And please give us credit for knowing that. There is nothing more ridiculous than some jackass who never saw two bulldogs fight expounding upon the "premeditated cruelty" of dogfighting.

Fact three: Dogfighting has gone on for as far back as we can see into the mists of ancient history, it is prevalent now, and it will continue to go on in the future. Stricter laws have not even slowed it down. (There has been an effect, though, and we will discuss that later.)

Fact four: At least ninety-five percent of A.P.B.T. owners do not fight their dogs. However, even people who want the dogs for some other purpose—even as just a house pet—want dogs from game stock. Thus, many a person has purchased a well-bred female, raised her up, paid the stud fee for a top sire, and produced a litter of representative Pit Bull pups without ever becoming involved in the fighting of dogs.

Fact five: In spite of stories to the contrary, deaths in the pit are extremely rare. While it is true that some dogs do die after a match (usually from improper treatment of hypovolemic shock), their longevity rate compares quite well with that of other performance breeds. (Stock dogs in Australia, for example, have an average life span of three years.) While non-game dogs are frequently put to sleep, the same thing is true of bird dogs that won't point. And many a hound has been "planted" merely because his voice (on the trail) did not suit his owner.

Fact six: There is no more relationship between pit fighting and violence than between pro football and violence. Any thinking

Riptide Becky, a Wallace female. This color is called "buckskin" by APBT fanciers.

Sequan Invictus undergoing the attack-training phase of Schutzhund training.

Gary Hammonds and Bruno (13 months old) in 1969.

person should realize that. The Pit Bull is popular because he is a truly heroic animal, and various devotees of the breed have stationed themselves at different distances from the actual pit fighting depending upon their own inclination. (Incidentally, for those that worry about pro football or even T.V. violence, there is some evidence recently reported that indicates that such things may act as a safety valve, and thus, make people less inclined to violence themselves.)

Now, with these facts in mind, we can view all the articles in perspective. Furthermore, taking these facts into consideration, isn't it ridiculous that various humane-oriented groups are pushing for felony laws for *intending* to fight these dogs (or even for fighting them, for that matter)? After all, simple assault on a human is not a felony. And if our critics are really concerned about the welfare of our dogs, they should be advised that the felony legislation they are pressing for in nearly every state is counterproductive to the welfare of the individual dogs. A felony law was passed in my state three years ago. It has not slowed down dogfighting in the state one iota. It has, however, caused some of the most reputable people to give up the dogs or to move out of the state. This trend results in our dogs being left in the hands of those who are not concerned about being lawbreakers. The net result is that, while dogfighting has not decreased, the quality of the people has deteriorated. Such people are more likely to neglect their dogs, and there are fewer people around to influence them otherwise.

The question is: Do the critics really have the welfare of our dogs at heart? It is a question about which I have serious doubts. Their almost gleeful eagerness to put Pit Bulls to death (for their own good, of course!) shakes my confidence in them. I have often wondered how humane groups could label the Pit Bull "vicious" and "unsuited for pets", yet adopt out animals that had bitten children as "good watchdogs." But from the point of view of a humaniac, a dog that is a danger to animals is to be despised much more than one that merely attacks human beings! Perhaps that attitude explains the hysterical vendetta by the critics and the shrill harangues against our beloved breed that appear regularly in the various press media.

THE CHICKEN CURE
Richard F. Stratton
(Pit Bull Gazette, August 1979)

Well, the San Diego Humane Society finally got a chance to show its teeth here recently when they finally got a conviction on someone for possessing dogs with the intent that they be used in a fighting exhibition. The felony conviction carries a maximum penalty of a year and a day in jail plus a 50,000-dollar fine. However, a judge in superior court who is used to sentencing muggers, murderers, rapists, and their ilk is just not going to be inclined to come down heavy on a dog fighter—regardless of any silly laws the legislators get stampeded into passing by a lot of idle rich and ill-informed old ladies! The judge reduced the sentence to a misdemeanor and suspended it. Well, needless to say, the Humane Society representatives were enraged, and at this point, they showed their true colors. They began to direct all their energies to getting a court order to have all the man's dogs destroyed.

Susan Oswald and Laramee (age 6 months).

Norrod's Iron Taffy, a five-time winner.

This would be a good time to point out that the Humane Society is by nature a political organization. Accordingly, it has a number of ways of making its influence felt. It gives awards to the district Attorney's office, and apparently all the judges are honorary members of the society. However, Judge Levenson, who presided in this case, was candidly puzzled by the society's attitude. He admitted to a feeling that the society was conducting a vendetta against the breed; however, he granted a court order to have the dogs destroyed. Under pressure from Defense Attorney Matt Lees, though, the judge stayed the execution of the order for ten days. He said he did not want to have the dogs destroyed, but he needed to be given an alternative.

Attorney Lees waged a courageous fight for the dogs. He obtained a list of over a hundred people that would offer homes and agree to inspection by the Humane Society. He also obtained a dog trainer to examine the animals and determine if they were suitable as pets. The Humane Society countered by sending their own "expert", a dog trainer and owner of the largest boarding kennel on the West Coast. The man's wife is on the board of directors of the Humane Society, so you can imagine just how objective

Wallace's Dude on the right as a pup. The pup on the left is Wallace's Fancy.

he was in his judgment! And, of course, the point should be made here that dog trainers are no more authorities on dogs than are dog fighters! The real experts are research scientists such as Scott and Fuller, who have been studying the behavior of dogs scientifically for many years.

The case ended suddenly when the judge signed an order to have the dogs destroyed. By the time the defense attorney heard about it, the dogs were already dead. The society had wasted no time. There was quite a bit of local television coverage. Attorney Matt Lees was interviewed and spoke forcefully and dramatically against the unseemly vendetta of the Humane Society and the fact that proper protocol had not been followed. The owner was interviewed and could not hide the tears caused by the sorrow of his dogs having to pay the price of his conviction. Obviously, the Humane Society did not reap very good publicity in this incident. And well that they did not, for I knew those dogs, and there was absolutely no excuse for their destruction. There was not a dog there that was a danger to any human. And some of them had been whelped right there in the Humane Society kennels.

When a dog kills a chicken, an old farm cure is to tie the chicken around the dog's neck. If I have my way, the Humane Society will not be able to forget its "kill" either. I plan to do my best to see to it that the ghosts of their victims come back to haunt them again and again. I, for one, would like to know why the Humane Society gives top priority to their vendetta against our dogs and lets unspeakable cruelties go by the boards! I am tired of the cowardly and furtive attitude of many of its officers who mouth their falsehoods to the media and in their private publications. I hereby challenge *any* Humane Society official to an open debate on the merit of these matters right here in the pages of this journal. Come on out of hiding, guys, and let's let the sun shine in!

LIZA ON THE ICE
Richard Stratton
(Pit Bull Gazette, Volume 2 No. 2)

Generally speaking, the dog men that have made a lasting contribution to the breed are the more reputable people, such as John

Hammonds' Bruno and Macho working the tire together—a tricky situation.

Opposite:
Wallace's Star.

P. Colby, W.R. Lightner, and Bob Wallace. The riff-raff contribute little of value, and they tend to become lost in the sands of antiquity. An exception, however, comes to mind in the person of Dan McCoy. He was an itinerant fry cook, usually working in the oil fields of Texas. He was famous for two things: his great knowledge of Pit Bulldogs and his enormous consumption of alcohol. When old time dog men get together, talk invariably swings around to McCoy and his antics, and each one has a different story to tell. The following is one of my favorites.

Around the turn of the century in the small town of Boulder, Colorado, an actor troupe had come to town to present the play *Uncle Tom's Cabin.* In those days it was the custom for traveling groups such as this to provide a little additional entertainment (such as vaudeville acts), and they often advertised their arrival with a parade. The parade for *Uncle Tom's Cabin* included two large and noisy Great Danes. These dogs played the part of the Bloodhounds that trailed Liza across the ice in the story the troupe was presenting. Apparently, true Bloodhounds were not menacing enough in appearance for the dramatic effect that the producers of the play desired, so they had substituted the Great Danes.

The giant dogs certainly looked formidable all right as they pulled on their leashes and bellowed at the people that lined the streets to watch the parade. One observer, however, was unimpressed; in fact, Dan McCoy chuckled to himself as he saw the dogs approaching and the people shrinking back as they passed by. McCoy slipped away to an alley a few blocks up from the parade. There behind a restaurant was stationed old "Denver," a 45-pound veteran of a number of pit contests. "Denver" was a comical-looking dog, white with a brindle saddle and a patch over one eye, but his fighting ability was substantial. McCoy unbuckled Denver's collar. He didn't have to point the way. Denver had heard the baying of the Great Danes.

The dogs in the parade had progressed to within a block of the restaurant when a tornado came charging at them from out of the crowd. Denver's arrival had the impact of an exploding artillery shell. One of the Great Danes was knocked off his feet, and the other was sent reeling toward the crowd. "Denver" concentrated his attention on the downed Dane, and the dog howled in pain and fright. McCoy, meanwhile, ran around in outraged indignation

178

A rare old photo of Tudor's Dibo, a dog who figures in the pedigree of just about every pure bred American Pit Bull Terrier of today.

The author with Going Light Barney.

demanding to know over and over again who had let old "Denver" loose. Well, the Great Danes were eventually saved, and "Denver" was returned to his quarters. The play was presented the next night, and from what I am told, it was well received. Of course, there were a few giggles from the audience when the hounds limped after Liza across the ice! Somehow they no longer seemed terribly awesome!

Sequan Jester, son of Going Light Jim.

Dickie and Nancy Freeman with Black Angel, a daughter of Dillinger out of Peterbilt's dam, Buton's Babe.

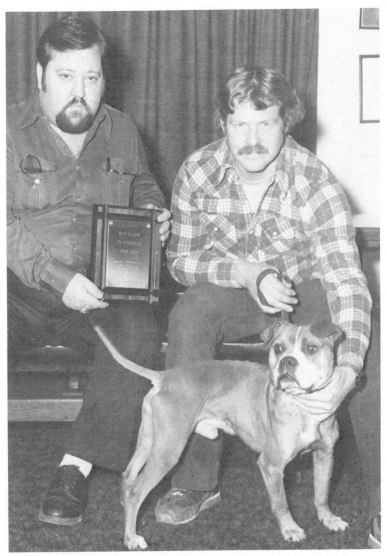

Dean Hudson (l.) and Dave Adams (r.) with their great little pit dog Champion Booker T.

Chapter 7

More Questions and Answers

*Curiosity is one of the permanent and certain
characteristics of a vigorous intellect.*

Samuel Johnson

For a time I wrote a question-and-answer column for
Bloodlines Journal. In my first book, I devoted a chapter to
some of the questions asked and my responses because I
knew that a lot of other novices would have the same questions. Now, for the same reason as before, I am including additional questions and the answers I gave.

Question: *Hypothetically, if you had a game Staff, would you
still consider it a separate breed?*

Fred Nemiroff
Brooklyn, NY

Answer: In my opinion, it should still be considered a separate breed, because statistically its progeny would not be
game. I know that some people are having a hard time going
along with the idea of the Staff being a separate breed. However, the definition of a breed is (in part) "having consistent
inherited characteristics," so from the point of view of
APBT enthusiasts, the Staff is a separate breed. The Staff
people, on the other hand, think in terms of appearance
alone, and consequently, regard the APBT as a Staff.

Sorrell's Crazy Mary III.

Sarona Motorhead, 48 pounds pit weight, is Clouse Stabber and Old Family Red Nose breeding.

Question: *Tell me, would you consider breeding a Pit Bull that you knew was not game just because the dog had good looks and conformation?*

Aygmund Matuszevski
Ontario, Canada

Answer: Absolutely not!

Question: *Are choke chains bad for a dog's throat?*

Lillian Rashell
Galena Park, TX

Answer: Probably not; however, they are dangerous to leave on a dog if he is tied up because the choke collar can hang in the "choke" position! Careful owners do not even leave the choke chain collars on their dogs even when they are running loose, because there is always the remote possibility that one of the rings of the collar could get caught on something. (Just for the record, I have a definite prejudice against choke collars)!

Question: *Regarding your article on Dibo: 1. I thought Heinzl had bred Dibo since he was out of Hubbard's Bounce and Heinzl's Bambi, but you said a man named Smith bred him. Could you explain this? 2. Why wasn't the breeding of Bounce and Bambi repeated after it was learned how Dibo produced?*

W.D. Pitrman
Redondo Beach, CA

Answer: 1. Smith was a novice breeder who had happened to obtain some good dogs. He either got Bambi from Heinzl or Ed Ritcheson (former partner of Heinzl's), and bred her to Bounce who was owned at the time by Wiz Hubbard. Bounce was a son of old Hubbard's Gimp. All of these dogs were down from an Old Family bloodline that had been preserved by Con Feeley, and later, after his death, by men who had known him. 2. By the time Dibo's quality and his great prepotency had been recognized, Bounce had been shipped to Joe Corvino, and we also have to take into account that the dogs were fairly old by this time, too. Bambi produced a number of good dogs bred to dogs other than Bounce, and Bounce produced some good ones bred to other bitches, too—like Rascal (to name just one!).

Sorrells' Red Jerry was a key dog in the foundation of the Sorrells line.

Sequan Mike, the dog with the bad heart, avoiding exertion on the springpole.

Opposite:
Norrod's Muhammed Ali, a two-time winner and
an example of the Old Family Red Nose strain.

189

Wallace's Jeff, who later
became known as Dodd's
Jeff.

Question: *Granting that inbreeding is a valuable breeding tool in the hands of an expert, why is it ever necessary to make an outcross?*

Earl Shockley
Butte, Montana

Answer: The main justification for an outcross is when we have lost something in our basic strain (*i.e.,* stamina). the outcross is the price we pay for not having been sufficiently selective with our stock.

Question: *Should the ears of an American Pit Bull Terrier be trimmed?*

Al Faulker
Hopkinsville, Tenn.

Answer: This is all a matter of personal preference. I am inclined to prefer the natural ears, but I have seen many dogs that I thought looked good with trimmed ears; however, I am one of those who do not mind diversity of appearance, as I have also seen dogs with docked tails that I thought looked pretty good, too! (Just for the record, though, most fanciers cannot abide a docked tail in the breed, but they are all fairly tolerant about ears.) I have heard people justify the cropping

190

Right: Skip McMichael and Hammonds' "D.C.", a Bruno-Heinzl bloodlines production. **Below:** Wallace's Peggy didn't look like she could whip a tomcat, but she was a powerhouse tornado and game to the core.

Susanka's Pits, owned by Mork Susanka.

Fonseca's Pinscher. Sire: Heinzl's Speck. Dam: Fancy.

Left: Hammonds' Dempsey sits atop an overturned water bucket. **Below:** Teddy Bear, a son of Chato and thereby a grandson of Wallace's Bad Red.

Another shot of Greenwood's Oakie.

of ears on the curious basis that it prevented ear cankers. Unfortunately, there apparently is no scientific basis for such a claim. The truth is the *only* justification for the cropping of the ears is the appearance that it produces, and you'll have to make your decision on that basis alone.

Question: *Since Bob Wallace was primarily renowned as a breeder of the Old Family Red Nose bloodlines, I was wondering where the brindle dogs came from (i.e., Wallace's Toney)?*

Bob Jurgens
Baltimore, Md.

Answer: Actually, Wallace maintained two basic strains, his original Wallace line and the Old Family Red Nose strain. Wallace's original line was based on Searcy Jeff (a brindle dog but the son of an Old Family Red Nose sire), Toney (a brindle and white dog), Penny (a Shipley bitch that came down from straight Corcoron blood), and Centipede (one of the original Old Family Red Nose greats). The old Wallace dogs were brindle, brindle and white, and occasionally red. Bob kept the Old Family Red Nose dog as a line to utilize as an outcross for his main line. In the latter part of his breeding career, Wallace also maintained the old Feeley line

A white Bull Terrier, one of the breeds recognized by the American Kennel Club which some people occasionally confuse with the American Pit Bull Terrier.

Opposite:
John Stratton, a son of the author, with Riptide Belle.

Left: Gus Brown's Lady, sired by a Heinzl dog out of a Colby bitch. **Below:** Cesar's Zorba, a one-time winner and very game, she was sired by Sorrells' Red Jerry out of Crazy Mary II.

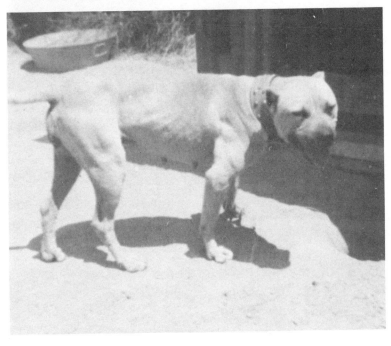

Right: The author in his college days with Mike, a Lightner dog. **Below:** Satan, a son of Zebo.

199

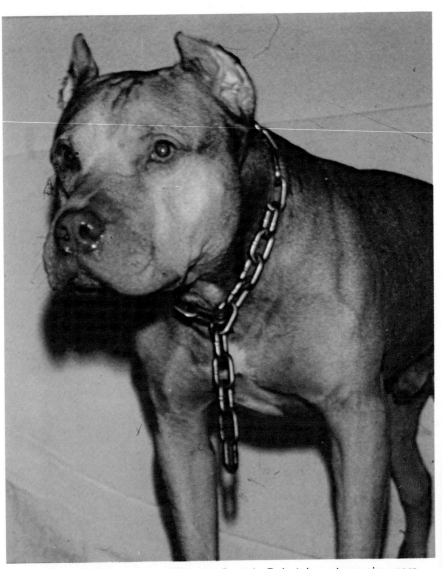

One of the last photos of Savage Captain Bob, taken at age six years.

Tom II.

for use as an outcross, but he never found the need to utilize it.

Question: *Your theory about the origin of the American (Pit) Bull Terrier makes sense, and most of the evidence supports it. One thing, however, troubles me. That is the variation of appearance in the breed. It seems to me that a breed that has had no outbreedings for hundreds of years would have a more uniform appearance.*

Richard A. Gibson
Oxnard, Tenn.

Answer: First of all, I would like to clarify that I would never want to claim that there have been absolutely NO outcrosses at all—ever! Breeds are only pure in a relative sense, and we can't make the claim that there have been no outcrosses whatsoever for any breed. I do challenge the idea that there have been any outbreedings that were deliberate and of significance to the breed. There are always rumors and stories, but I think we can safely disregard them. It is always easy to start rumors about a breed or strain. A recent one that I find particularly amusing is that the "Eli" line was founded by a cross to a Labrador Retriever! As for the disparity in appearance, we must remember that we get what we breed for, and there has been very little attempt to breed for a particular type in the American (Pit) Bull Terrier breed. Consequently, whatever features the APBT has that give it a "type" are functional features (*e.g.,* a large head to provide large and powerful jaws). Obviously, these features are fairly flexible and can be compensated for by other traits (also functional and variable). These variable and functional features do give the American (Pit) Bull Terrier somewhat of a uniform appearance—but within broad parameters. It should be noted that some of the most valuable and highly respected performance breeds (Border Collie, Queensland Heeler, etc.) have a variable appearance, but they are much more highly bred than most show dog breeds.

202

Question: *Doesn't the very name of the American Pit Bull Terrier confirm that the breed was formed by a cross of the Bulldog with a terrier of some sorts?*

Milton Brammer
Sioux City, Iowa

Answer: Not really. The Bull Terrier was a "top hat" that was used for our breed in print only for many years because show dogs were called that. But they were still known as "Bulldogs" among people that raised them. The readers may be interested to know that the breed was simply called "Bull Terrier" by people that thought the (English) Bull Terrier was the show version of our breed. Later "pit" was added to distinguish the breed from the "bench type" (which was actually the English Bull Terrier—a separate breed). Still later, "American" was added to further separate the two breeds in people's minds, partly because the Bull Terrier folks started to refer to their charges as "Pit Bull Terriers", too.

Question: *Why is the "pit" in the APBT name placed in parentheses?*

Milton Brammer
Sioux City, Iowa

Answer: At one time the American Pit Bull Terrier was formally referred to by three separate names: Bull Terrier, Pit Bull Terrier, and American Bull Terrier. Finally the three names were incorporated together, and the "Pit" was placed in parentheses to show that it was optional. Personally, I am in favor of dropping the parentheses, as they are cumbersome to use. Also, since no one seems to be using the name " 'American' Bull Terrier" any longer they no longer have a valid function.

Question: *I notice a tendency among some APBT breeders to breed very large dogs, 70 and 80 pounds or more. I also know that most of the really game old-time imported dogs from Ireland were small, in the 30 and 40 pound class. Do you think it is*

Jimmy Boots, shown at close to ideal pit weight.

Hammonds' Minnie, Pure Heinzl breeding out of Bud and Taffy.

Left: C. B. Jurgens and Jurgens' Mariner, better known as "Butch." **Right:** Saddler's Mike is right at pit weight (45 lbs) with George Saddler in the background. Saddler was one of the most knowledgeable of dog men. **Below:** Greenwood's Champion Our Gal Sunday, now owned by Andre Giroux.

Girley Crum's Taffy, a Carver-bred bitch.

possible to retain the gameness while increasing the size?
Marvin Parker
Springfield Garden, NY

Answer: Generally speaking, the larger dogs do not run as game as the smaller ones. Gameness is not really related to size, per se; however, the most reputable and capable breeders have usually had a definite predilection for smaller dogs. Hence, the smaller dogs have usually been better bred.

Question: *My wife and I are fairly new to the APBT scene. We now own two APBT's and want to get into showing them. We would appreciate, as I'm sure others would, knowing what the majority of judges look for in the show dogs. We would also appreciate some clarification of the breed standard. Thank you.*
Tom and Lynn May
Fontana, California

Stratton's Boozer (age 4 months), a descendant of O'Brian.

Opposite:
Nancy and Dickie Freeman with
Honeybear.

Answer: Those who read my column regularly know that I am the wrong man to talk to about dog shows! I would suggest you contact the Golden State Pit Bull Club, P.O. Box 5186, Buena Park, California 90620. In spite of my rotten attitude about dog shows, this organization has seen fit to honor me with a life membership, for which I sincerely thank them. They also have considerable experience at showing dogs, and I am sure that they would be most willing to be of help to anyone that is interested in that area of endeavor.

Question: *I got your book and loved it! It has really whetted my appetite for other books that have been written on the breed. Are any of them available?*

Jim Mylee
Clarksville, Tennessee

Answer: Walter H. Patton, Jr., who puts out a bi-monthly newsletter for the American Staffordshire Terrier Association for Fanciers, lists the following books:
1. *The American Pit Bull Terrier* (Colby) $13.00
2. *Memories of the Pit* (Meeks) $14.00
3. *Pit Rules* $8.00
4. *The Dog Pit (Fox) $8.00*

Question: *What are the physical differences between a Staff and a Pit Bull?*

Irene Case
Monkato, MN

Answer: (Sigh!) Generally speaking, the A.P.B.T. is higher stationed, has a slightly more narrow head, and has a slightly looser (and tougher!) hide than the Staff. However, to be perfectly candid, there is no foolproof way of distinguishing the breeds by sight alone that will be effective one hundred percent of the time.

Question: *Do you have a second favorite breed?*

Emily Stroud
Baltimore, Maryland

Answer: Yes, I think that probably either the Redbone or Bluetick Coonhound would be a second-favorite dog for me. Also in the running would be the Border Collie, the Labrador Retriever, and the Brittany Spaniel. Although most of the dogs I selected are hunting dogs, I am not a hunter. It is just that I appreciate dogs with unique abilities more than I do dogs that have an exotic appearance.

Question: *Could the A.P.B.T. survive in the wild?*

Steve Mitchel
Utica, NY

Answer: Probably not, for two reasons. First, the short coat would not provide adequate protection from the elements. Second, most A.P.B.T.'s would waste valuable food gathering time and expose themselves to danger needlessly. But other domestic dogs would have similar problems. For example, a hound would also fritter away its time by trailing animals continuously, a retriever would carry around sticks and perhaps waste his time swimming, a sheepdog would herd antelope, etc. The point is that all of our domestic functional breeds are specialists of sorts. The wild canines are basically eating and procreating machines. We have added an extra dimension to our domestic breeds by selective breeding. For example, a Border Collie finds great joy in herding sheep, and will often even ignore a female in heat when so occupied. A retriever is fascinated by flying things and has an irresistible urge to retrieve objects that fall from the sky. A bird dog thinks that birds are absolutely the most fascinating things in the world. And a Pit Bull thinks that dogs are! Now these extra dimensions may provide added pleasure for the breeds involved, but they are obtained only by a program of selective breeding that frees the animals from the demands of its natural environment, and in turn places new demands on it. To put the idea of *any* breed's surviving in the wild into perspective, it is instructive to note that even wild canines removed from the wild for a period of time may not survive

Sarona Trouble, a modern example of a good Old Family Red Nose dog.

Sorrell's Crazy Dugan, after his win over Stinson's Cannonball. Sire: Wallace's Talking Boy. Dam: Sorrell's Crazy Mary II.

Champion Driller was sired by the great dog Eli and was out of the great bitch Glory Bee.

if returned to their habitat because of interrupted social interaction and the possible modification of essential learned behavior patterns.

Question: *Is it true that the United Kennel Club intends to deny registration of inbred dogs. If so, I certainly do protest!*

Joe W. Oshburn
Oklahoma City, OK

Answer: It is my impression that the United Kennel Club is discouraging inbreeding by *amateur* breeders, and with good reason, for inbreeding has its pitfalls. However, expert breeders in many areas (hunting dogs, guide dogs and herding dogs) have utilized inbreeding extensively as an invaluable tool for fixing desired traits. Inbreeding can also be utilized to purify a strain of undesirable characteristics and diseases.

Question: *I would very much appreciate any information about the different bloodlines, or any advice on getting an American (Pit) Bull Terrier that is not game.*

Matthew M. Colopy
Portsmouth, VA

Answer: It is difficult to be of much help here, for all bloodlines have their good and bad dogs. And the popularity of the different strains has a tendency to run in cycles. Sometimes strains that are rich in tradition and quality are allowed to become extinct, unfortunately. Such was the fate of the Diamond Dick and Henry bloodlines. Right now the Corvino line is riding the crest of current popularity. In the next decade, it will probably be some other strain. I know for a fact that some of the advertisers in *Bloodlines* produced some great dogs. I can testify to the quality of dogs coming from the strains of Boudreaux, Heinzl, McCaw, and of course, I have my own personal preference for the Wallace and Old Family Red Nose strains. One thing I can guarantee, however. Regardless of the strain you select, you will still get plenty of the kind that are not too game!

Question: *At our club shows, the Staffs, since they are bred for conformation, usually win over the American Pit Bull Terriers. Obviously, this is a bad situation, but what is the solution? Should the standard be changed?*

Bob Lesnik
Fair Lawn, NJ

Answer: The problem with a standard is that, regardless of how well it is written, it can be interpreted "or bent" enough to go along with the style of the moment. The current style with Staffs overemphasizes a heavy head and a blocky build.

Hemphill's Reckless Red II appears in many pedigrees, especially those dogs that are descended from the old red nose strain.

Opposite:
Blackjack and Gary Sampler,
summer of 1974.

Norrod's Iron Spike, a four-time winner and grandson of Ross's Red
Devil.

Marshall's Lady was sired by Syke's Butcher and won several matches.

That doesn't mean that some very fine Pit Bulls don't come that way, but generally speaking, the good ones are much higher stationed. The long legs provide for superior leverage, agility, and heat dissipation. The old Pit Bull is far and away the very best in his area of specialization, and for that reason, it is patently absurd to think of improving him in terms of a standard. The only answer at all to your dilemma that I can think of is for your club to select a judge who is thoroughly familiar with the APBT, and is not Staff oriented.

Question: *If your book does not discuss important dogs such as Dibo and Rascal, why should I buy it?*

Name Withheld

Answer: The book was not intended to be an encyclopedia. It merely has sections which are intended to provide glimpses of the breed for those who are not too familiar with it. Some outstanding dogs were covered, but many outstanding and significant individuals were neglected out of necessity. While the book is not intended to teach or instruct those who are already thoroughly familiar with the breed, it has re-

218

ceived high praise from some old timers, and was ordered by some of the most reputable breeders in the country.

Question: *Do you think the ears of an APBT should be cropped?*

Gerald Almy
Tyler, TX

Answer: That depends on the time of day, the angle of the sun in the sky, and my mood of the moment! Seriously, although I fluctuate as to whether to trim ears or not, I lean slightly toward natural ears.

Question: *Regarding the gameness of the American Staffordshire Terrier, I have a Pit Bull, but I sold a Staff to a guy who uses him for boar hunting, and he really goes after those hogs. Isn't that gameness?*

Jim Toledo
Ft. Worth, TX

Answer: Okay, one more time around the mulberry bush on this one! I have tried to stress that the American Staffordshire Terrier should be considered a different breed because of a difference in expectations in terms of deep gameness. Fighting a boar or a bull (or a lion for that matter!) does not necessarily test deep gameness. Now, of all the things I have written, I think saying that the American Staffordshire Terrier should no longer be considered an American Pit Bull Terrier is the thing that has upset the most people. But, it is hardly a novel point of view. For over thirty years, the most reputable Pit Bull breeders have held the same opinion. However, both the United Kennel Club and the American Dog Breeders Association register Staffs as APBT's. And to be perfectly frank, I don't find the situation to be more than mildly alarming. The top breeders usually will not even breed outside their own strain, let alone to a Staff! So it is difficult to see the harm in it all. I have stated the facts as I see them for their academic interest more than anything else, and I am not on an anti-Staff or anti-show campaign.

"PR" Apache Tiger Lil. Sire: Wise's Maximillian. Dam: Wise's Terrible Tippy.

Wise's Dark Hazzard (age 9 months); also known as Apache Dark Hazzard. Sire: Divine's Deuce (Larry Coleman's). Dam: "PR" Wise's Sugar Babe.

Clinton Farrell with his
wife (l.) and their friend
pictured with Farrell's
Dugan.

Question: *Last September our son flew in from San Francisco
bringing a treasured gift, an American (Pit) Bull Terrier. Without a doubt this dog is the most affectionate, joyful, and energet-
ic pet we've ever owned. We are concerned about her encounters
with other dogs. In the event of a fight, how do we break her hold
to keep her from killing another dog?*

Thomas A. Nutter
Warren, Indiana

Answer: First of all, not all Pit Bulls (especially females)
develop an urge to fight—especially if you avoid confronta-
tions with other dogs. If you don't want your dog to be a
fighter, the cardinal rule with a Pit Bull is not to let him get
a taste of it. If your dog develops the urge to fight other dogs
(even without encounters), then you simply have to keep
your dog on leash and separated from other dogs. Now of
course, it is possible to "condition" the Pit Bull not to fight
by use of an electric stinger. In the case of our breed, this
amounts to malconditioning, and you usually end up with an
unhappy animal. To break your dog's hold, you can choke
her off or use a breaking stick. The latter is the preferred and
humane method.

Possibly one of the greatest ever, the immortal Boomerang—a grand champion and three times best in show.

Question: *For those of us looking for a stud dog, what is the best dog in the country to go to with a female?*

Joe Washington
Bowling Green, Ky.

Answer: Well, that partly depends on the female and her breeding. As for picking the top stud dogs, I can only recommend the ones I know something about, but going in alphabetical order, I would recommend the following: Alligator, Alvin, Art, Barney, Boomerang, Bull, Drummer, Gringo, Hank, Jeremiah, Jessie, and Roger, to name just a few.

Question: *Which is most important in transmitting gameness, the stud dog or brood bitch?*

David Benett
Newark, N.J.

Hammonds' Bruno the beggar.

Answer: They both transmit an equal number of genes.

Question: *What strain of American Pit Bull Terriers is the best?*

Al Jensen
Great Falls, Montana

Answer: No one strain is best, but the so-called Dibo line is obviously the most popular now.

Question: *What is the difference between the Old Family Red dogs and the Old Family Red Nose dogs?*

Joseph Bishop
Chicago, IL

Answer: The terms are generally used synonymously, but strictly speaking, they are not the same. There are three designations to get straight here: (1) The Old Family refers to a strain of the old Irish dogs, generally small, very highly bred, and renowned for their gameness. (2) The Old Family Reds were a segment of the Old Family that consisted of generally red dogs or red and white dogs. They weren't bred for color, but the dominant colors (brindle, black, etc.) had been lost in this closely-bred strain. (The Gashouse dogs stemmed, in the main, from this family.) (3) The Old Family Red Nose is a segment of the Old Family Red strain that tended to show a red (or copper-colored) nose.

Question: *You spoke of the Dibo and Heinzl strains. Wasn't Dibo a product of Heinzl's breeding?*

Al Royce
Conrad, MT

Answer: Yes. However, it is common practice to speak of certain segments of strains by using the name of an individual dog. Dibo is particularly significant because of his prepotency as a stud dog. If the technical definition of a strain is a "variety within a variety", then I suppose a segment within a strain would be "a variety within a variety within a variety"!

Question: *Why do people inbreed if it is such a bad thing?*

Dave Silkwood
Birmingham, AL

Answer: Well, I certainly challenge the notion that inbreeding *per se* is a bad thing. All the great successful projects in history—from guide dogs to herding dogs—have utilized inbreeding extensively. What inbreeding does is to give the breeder more control by closing off and reducing the size of the genetic pool with which he is working. In such a situation there is a slide toward recessive traits, because the dominants, once discarded, are lost. Some recessive traits are desirable and some are not (certain mental and physical disorders being the most notorious of the undesired traits). It should be of interest here to note that it is actually "outbreeding" that perpetuates nearly all of these undesirable recessive traits, even though they turn up only rarely. In an intense inbreeding program, the breeder should expect some bad characteristics to show up, but if he is consistent about culling them out from his breeding program, the breeder, after a few generations, will have a strain that is purified of all these undesirable traits. I believe that the emphasis should be on *selection* in any selective breeding program. There is a vast difference between the haphazard breeder who breeds daughter to father merely out of convenience and the systematic breeder who makes the same type of breeding, but after years of careful selection and planning.

Question: *Is it true that hounds are better kill dogs in the hunt than a Pit Bull?*

Paul Shockly
Mt. Home, AR

Answer: No. Hounds are marvelous animals, but their specialty is trailing and giving voice on the trail. All knowledgeable dog men are aware that the Pit Bull is the fighter deluxe and absolutely fearless regardless of the size of the animal. Now, many gentle people may wonder what on earth other

Gaboon Trahan and the famous bitch Black Widow. A poor photograph of a great animal.

folks (many of *us* gentle people, too!) would want with such a fighting machine. The truth is, of course, that the A.P.B.T. has other qualities, too. But, let's be honest, we all appreciate the A.P.B.T.'s ability. The point is that there is no need for the A.P.B.T. to be a threat to innocent animals if he is owned by a responsible person. No one should expect a dog to be discriminating about an overwhelming inborn urge—although, amazingly, some of them are! As a boy, I had been given a "schooled-out" pit dog, and he never bothered a dog that didn't bother him.

Hammonds' Reginald from "Rufus" bred to Trussell and Howard's Midget. Littermate to Matson's Goose and Anderson's Smiley.

Chapter 8

Breathing Life into the Legend

*I cannot tell how the truth may be; I say the
tale as 'twas said to me.*

Scott

I have been gratified by the comment on my first book by
many experienced Bulldog people. More than one has said
that they make the book required reading for would-be puppy buyers if they have not had a Bulldog before. So often I
have been told that the book is the next best thing to owning
an American Pit Bull Terrier. If there was a specific chapter
that was singled out for praise, it was the one titled "Short
and Tall Tales of the Pit Bull." I think these stories provided individual "snapshots" of various aspects of the nature
of the breed. It was probably this chapter more than any of
the others that made the book "the next best thing to owning
a Bulldog". Scores of people have requested that I include a
similar chapter in my new book. Okay, folks, this is it!

GETTING ON THE STICK

As most people that have owned Bulldogs know, the breed
is generally one that is very toy-oriented. This stems quite
naturally from its natural playfulness and enthusiasm. Even
chain dogs and kennel dogs find items to utilize for play,
such as logs, bones or rocks. Part of this behavior, of course,
stems from the breed's urge for fighting contact; hence, they
"fight" their doghouses, logs, rocks and whatever. It is not
unusual to see a Bulldog hanging six feet in the air from a

Left: Riptide Buckboard, one of the last of the Wallace dogs, plays with a block of wood. **Below:** Another look at "Pooch Patch" (Howard Heinzl's place) and one of the reverend's favorite dogs, Heinzl's Chile.

230

four-by-four overhang in his kennel! Basically, however, whatever they do is all in the spirit of play and every Pit Bulldog I've ever owned was a natural retriever of whatever you wanted to throw.

In this story Pat, a tan-spotted white dog, was a "stick dog." His owners had played tug-of-war with him, utilizing a stick, since the time he was a puppy. He became so taken with sticks that he was constantly on the lookout for one. If you picked up a stick, Pat's eyes lit up in excitement and locked in on that stick. Quick as a cat and strong as a mountain lion, the dog would have hold of the stick and commence his game of trying to take it away. This usually didn't take long for although Pat only weighed 45 pounds, few people were able to hold on to that stick as the dog shook it and went through a repertoire of gyrations to wrest it away. Once having obtained his prize, the dog paraded around the yard waving it high in the air for everybody to see, all the time wagging his tail and looking back as if to say, "Aha, I got it away from you again!" After a minute or two he would bring the stick back to get the game started all over.

One time an older fellow (about my age!) came to visit Pat's owners. As he entered the front gate, Pat, in his role of official greeter, came running from the back of the house. As so many people do, our visitor detected a menace that wasn't there. He reached down, picked up a stake and held it over his head to warn the dog away. Now at that particular point in time, there just was nothing our visiting uncle could have done that would have been so completely wrong! Pat ran up the side of the terrified man, secured the stick in his jaws and after a spectacular display of mid-air gyrations, shook the stake loose from the man and landed on the ground about the same time as the man landed on his back. We can only imagine the relief of the avuncular visitor to see the dog prance off content with merely the stick in his mouth and leaving our friend with his scalp intact!

A week or two later the boys were relating the incident to a burly friend. Failing to see the humor in the story, the friend said if he'd had the stick he would have driven that dog into the next neighborhood. One thing led to another and finally the boys handed their mesomorphic friend the stick and let him try to drive the dog off. The young braggart ran at Pat (who had been snoozing) with the stick. Pat awoke with delight—someone new to play the game with! Ignoring the barrage of blows (and taking no offense at them), Pat soon had the stick in his grasp. Holding the stick in an iron grip, Pat wrapped his forelegs around the boy's arm, at the same time pushing with all his might against the boy's armpit and neck with his hind legs. After a couple of sharp twists, Pat had his prize and was doing his victory dance around the yard, waving aloft his beloved stick! Pat's merriment was contrasted by the befuddlement of the youth who simply could not believe he had been "disarmed" so quickly by *any* dog, let alone such a small one.

SPANKY AND HUTCH

In the wilds of Arkansas there live my good friends, Casey Jones (no, not an engineer, but an attorney!) and his beautiful wife, Janet. For years they kept two grown male Pit Bulldogs together in the house. The dogs had been raised together and got along beautifully. Oh, there was one small problem. It seems that Hutch could turn doorknobs, regardless of their size or configuration. It took a while before the Jones' figured out who had been letting their dogs out! In spite of warnings to the contrary to Casey and Janet by Bulldog people, the two male dogs got along beautifully. But a day of reckoning was coming!

Naturally, it had to happen when Janet was alone at home, but it could have been worse. It could have happened when no one was there! As it was, pint-sized Janet was faced with the task of trying to separate two 60-pound Bulldogs going at it hammer and tongs all through the house. Why the dogs suddenly started fighting remains a mystery. And to poor,

Indian Eddie's Gigi was sired by Koehler's (Sorrells') Bull and whelped by Koehler's Josie.

horrified Janet, it was academic. I am sure she thought the dogs were going to kill each other, as they tumbled from one room to another while poor Janet struggled vainly to separate them. At the end of twenty minutes, Janet was more tired than the dogs! She was finally able to get a door wedged between the two tiring animals and pulled Hutch into a bathroom, leaving Spanky outside. Then Janet sat down on the floor struggling to get her breath back. Then, before her horrified eyes, the doorknob turned, the door swung open and in came Hutch headed on the run for Spanky!

CRUISER MISTAKEN FOR MILKBONE

The following story appeared in a number of California newspapers and also appeared on television. I will just paraphrase a news clipping that was sent to me by Lou Diehl. As Lou said, this was "another tall tale that turned out to be true".

According to the report two Pit Bulldogs were in custody in the Santa Clara County Animal Shelter, charged with chewing the tires off a Sunnyvale police car while an embarrassed policeman was trapped in the car. The patrolman didn't want to talk about the encounter with the 35-pound dogs—Lady, three years old and her son Isaac, two.

An animal control officer had to stop laughing to discuss the scene he was called to Sunday morning. "There was this patrol car in the middle of the intersection with its red lights on and it had one flat tire in front, with a hubcap lying in the road, and two Pit Bulldogs chewing on the back tires, and I saw all the tires go flat. The officer couldn't get out of the car".

When he got out of the truck, the animal control officer said the dogs ran toward him. However, they ran off into their yard when he hollered at them. The owner of the house said he had no idea the dogs were loose. "They're friendly dogs," he said. "They just don't like uniforms".

According to the police report the police officer had been cruising in Sunnyvale when he saw the unleashed dogs. He got out of his car to investigate and was chased back into his vehicle. The owner was cited for allowing his dogs to run about without a leash. The dogs are being held until their owner pays for the tires.

THE B FACTOR

One of the attributes of the Pit Bull that I have touted has been the capacity of the breed to resist disease or to bounce back from injury. Of course, Bulldogs do get sick like other dogs, but they seem to have an ability to fight off most ailments and they can at times appear downright indestructible. The stories of Mike and Josh help illustrate this "bulletproof" nature of the breed.

Mike is owned by Bill and Gail Ross. During a routine puppy examination, a veterinarian discovered a very serious malformation of the heart. The predictions of doom were so dire that the Ross' took Mike to one of the top veterinarian colleges in the country in the hope of attaining the latest treatment. Mike was subjected to an exhaustive series of

234

Daniel's Tom, a four-time pit winner, was sired by a son of Sherrer's Candy and whelped by Boudreaux's Glory Bee.

tests. After a thorough screening of the dog and exploration of all possible avenues of treatment, the veterinarians and research scientists at the university had to give the bad news to Mike's owners. So serious was Mike's heart condition that, at best, he would only live to see his third birthday and that would be it. But, at least, they had some good news too. When Mike did go, it would be instantaneous and painless.

Everything considered, the Ross' took the news in stride. They decided to give Mike a short happy life; hence, they would not limit his activity. He was allowed to run and even work the springpole. When Mike was in his kennel run, he spent a good deal of his time leaping like a flying squirrel in order to see over the sides and look at the other dogs. Mike was so active and his health seemed so good that the Ross' began to wonder: could all that exercise have improved his heart? Unfortunately not, for the veterinarian rechecked everything and his heart was just as bad as ever. Apparently, however, there was a "b" factor at work here that no one was taking into account, not the Ross' and not the doctors. What was the "b" factor? Why the Bulldog factor, of course. That

235

ought to be worth at least a couple of extra years. At this point Mike is approaching his sixth birthday and is active as ever, but his heart still checks out terrible!

Now, as for Josh, he was a dog that Morrie Rootberg obtained from Joe Corvino. He was in my last book too, as the dog that held the policeman captive for several minutes. When Josh was a young dog, he contracted the dread disease of leptospirosis. It was especially bad in those days, as veterinarians of that time were more limited both in diagnostic tools and therapeutic methods. Most cases of leptospirosis were lost because they were diagnosed too late and the therapy available was limited. The veterinarian informed Morrie that Josh's chances were not good and that even if he did make it, he would never be the same dog again. Well, again everybody was neglecting the "b" factor. Not only did Josh survive, but he returned to full bloom of health. So amazed was the veterinarian that whenever the local veterinary association hosted seminars, Morrie was asked to bring Josh down for the visiting practitioners to see a dog that had completely recovered from a full-blown case of leptospirosis.

TOUGH TEST FOR COONS

The readers may note that I have drawn on Morrie Rootberg for a number of stories about Bulldogs. Pit dog men often look down their noses at anyone who has never matched dogs. To be fair to the pit dog men, there is a certain justification in their attitude, for, so often, people that have never matched a dog are abysmally ignorant about certain aspects of the breed. Sometimes, however, some pit dog men are surprisingly ignorant, too, about certain aspects of the breed. In any case Morrie, who has owned Bulldogs all his life but only one at a time, is one of those rare individuals who is quite well versed on all aspects of the American Pit Bull Terrier.

One reason Morrie has better-than-average knowledge about the breed is that he has a curious and analytical mind.

Girley Crum's Reno, a young son of the great bitch Cremator.

He never misses a chance to learn something new about dogs, whether it be from a veterinarian or a hound dog man. It seems that a particular hound man had told Morrie that a coon on a one-to-one basis could whip any dog. Morrie had a chance to test this idea when his dog Booger (sire of Going Light Barney) ran across a coon in a water and forest area in the midst of Chicago. The coon didn't even try to run. He was a big boar and had apparently taken his toll of dogs, for he showed absolutely no fear. That was his mistake, for Booger charged right in and promptly killed the coon. Poor Morrie didn't have his breaking stick, so he had to let Booger carry the coon home, and all the way he chewed on the coon and cracked bone after bone. By the time they reached home the raccoon resembled a bear rug. Hardened pit dog man that he was, Morrie kept Booger on a leash from that point on when they were in the raccoon area.

Sarona Buccaneer, a Wallace dog, that got loose by accident when he was a young dog and was killed in a kennel fight.

Chapter 9
The Keep

"Labor conquers all things."

Homer

Like the rest of this book, this chapter about the care and training of a fighting dog is for the information of the general public and is not intended as a handbook for potential pit dog men. For that reason no specific and detailed keep will be given. This chapter should be of interest even to those who are opposed to the matching of dogs, for it is the inside story of how pit dogs are trained.

Contrary to the ravings of many humaniacs, there is no need to train the American Pit Bull Terrier to want to fight. However, the desire of a young dog to fight will come to various dogs at different stages of maturation. Thus, some pups will fight at just a few weeks of age with such intensity that they must be broken apart with the use of breaking sticks. Others are quite mellow and show no desire to fight until they are three years old or even older. And strange as it may seem, there seems to be no correlation between how soon a dog starts and the depth of his gameness. Another variation is the outward passion shown by individual dogs. One dog can be an embarrassment to take for a walk because whenever he sees a dog, even if it is five blocks away, he turns into a screaming maniac! A more typical Pit Bull will make no sound when he sees a dog, but he will strain hard in his harness to get to him. Many of the best pit dogs were easy-going dogs that would ignore street dogs, or any dogs, except when faced against them in a pit. So again we have a situation in which there is no correlation, that is between aggressiveness (or craziness!) and gameness. Some of the great dogs of all time, Dibo, Centipede, Searcy Jeff and White Rock, were easy-going dogs that were not of the super aggressive type. However, in the pit they were veritable tornados, boring in hard, pushing the other dog into the boards and shaking with a vengeance.

While dogs differ in that they start at different ages, there also will be some that will never start at all, and there is no way to start them. They will let a dog chew on them and maybe even wag their tail while he does it! Fewer females than males start and females are a little more erratic than males, perhaps due to their heat cycle. Here, though, is an interesting point. Some dog men believe that the only reason there are more good males than females is because there has been more selectivity in regard to the males. Many more females than males are bred without being tested.

Another point of interest is whether or not gameness is connected to the sex drive. Well, my own view is that it absolutely is not, no more so than the desire to run in a greyhound! I think that idea originated among game chicken men. A fighting chicken can be castrated and he will eventually lose all desire to fight once the hormones have been washed out of his body. However, Pit Bulls have been altered and spayed with no effect on either gameness or fighting desire. The amusing point here is that quite often the operation was done on the advice of a veterinarian to curb the fighting urge in someone's pet Pit Bull. Well, it may work with other dogs but not these!

Anyway, given the fact that different dogs start at different ages, how does the typical pit dog man proceed? One method widely used is to walk an aggressive-acting dog by the young dogs on a daily basis. Now, with most dog men, the young dogs will be at least sixteen to eighteen months old. Some of

Butch House's Grand Champion Joker, with five wins, logged in lots of hours in a keep, and you can bet he loved every minute of it.

the dogs may shy away from the older and more aggressive dog. Others will try to play with him, while still others will fire up and act like they want to fight. Whatever the reaction, our pit dog man will not allow any contact for several days. Finally after a few days of going through this routine, he may allow contact between the older dog and one of the more aggressive-acting young dogs. He will allow the pup to be rolled for about five minutes and then break it up. A few weeks later the pup will be taken off his chain and taken to the pit for a short roll. And so it goes, step by careful step, the dog is "schooled." His schooling consists solely of a few short rolls against dogs with a variety of styles so that he may learn how to counter each of them. The pit dog man tries to make sure each roll is a pleasant experience because this is a confidence-building stage. For that reason, the young dog is not allowed to become overly tired and he is never put against overly rough opponents. There comes a time, though, when everything possible is done to discourage the young prospect. This is the game test and it is done after the schooling is completed. In a game test our young dog is typically put on a larger, rougher opponent. By this time our pit dog man knows how much pit intelligence, wrestling ability and biting power his young charge possesses. In the game

Ray McLean's Cisco demonstrates proper form for running the tread-mill. Again, this is a slat-type mill the only disadvantage of which is that it sounds like a passing freight train!

test he is endeavoring to probe the depth of his gameness, endurance and ability to take punishment. For that reason a game test is likely to last as long as an hour. There is variation of opinion here, though. Some dog fighters, if they like the way a young dog looks in a roll, will let a match be his game test. Ultimately, that's what a match is anyway: a game test for the elite of the American Pit Bull Terrier world.

Just as there are a small percentage of football players that will make it in professional ball, so, too, is there only a small percentage of Pit Bulls that will be good enough for the pit. If our prospect passes his game test, he is finally ready to match.

Before a match is made, a typical dog man has pulled his dog's weight down and experimented a bit to ascertain what is his most efficient fighting weight. Just as with boxers or wrestlers, this will be the lightest weight at which he retains full strength. There are two reasons for bringing down the weight. One, for the same rea son as in boxing or wrestling, is to keep from going against a larger opponent. Then there are the physiological reasons, such as too much fat being an extra burden on the circulatory system. Heat dissipation is an important factor here too. In any case once the pit weight is determined, the typical dog fighter then submits it at a match site or announces informally to other dog men that he has that particular weight open. Once the match is made, the dog goes into a keep.

"Keep" is a term that originally referred to the diet for use during the training of a fighting dog. It has since come to be applied more broadly; in fact, it is generally used to refer to every aspect of the keep, the diet, method of exercise, method of increasing the work for the dog, the number of times a dog is weighed a day and so on. There are almost as many different types of keeps as there are pit dog men, and each one naturally thinks he has the best and is inclined to keep at least portions of it secret. A typical keep, though, begins with a complete physical examination by a veteri narian. A full blood screening is done and the animal is checked for parasites.

Once cleared medically, the dog is again brought down to pit weight and begins his training. The key is to start out gradually, for it is easy to overdo, as the dog is usually a capable and willing worker. Too much work, however, can cause bloody or sore footpads. The footpads must be constantly watched and treated continually either with home concoctions or some commercial foot toughener. What kind of work do the dogs do? Again it varies with the individual dog man (and dog).

The springpole and treadmill used to be the stock-in-trade of the pit dog man. The springpole, however, is rarely used now as part of a serious conditioning program. In my opinion there is really nothing wrong with springpole work; it is just one of those things that has fallen out of favor. Potential back injuries and possible damage to the teeth are usually cited as reasons for not using the springpole. I've never had any of those problems with any of my dogs using the spring-pole; however, if I ever matched a dog I probably wouldn't use it either, simply because it is no longer in fashion! The treadmill is still used as part of a conditioning program but not as much as it once was.

The apparatus known as the "catmill" or "training machine" (a more archaic term) is very much in vogue now. There used to be prejudice against this piece of equipment, too, with people saying that it would injure the dog. Modern dog men, however, apparently feel that they have learned to

Sequan Tugger works the springpole.

use it properly. A lot of room is needed for the catmill, as it consists of a steel arm about ten feet long to which the dog is harnessed. Then there has to be a counterbalancing arm ten feet in the opposite direction. In addition there is usually an arm that supports a cage into which a cat, coon or possum can be placed as enticement to get the dog to run well. The caged animal (usually a cat) gets used to his role in the training and quite often will go to sleep, all the while being turned at a furious pace on his "merry-go-round"! Now you would think the dog would soon realize that his pursuit is a hopeless one; the faster he runs, the faster the cage retreats. Well, of course, even the dumbest of dogs will soon learn that he will never catch his prey, but the image excites him and makes him want to work harder. It is not unlike the fantasies that marathon runners use to keep going or that football players utilize to get "psyched up" for a game. Anyway, most pit dogs are such bears for work that they will work the catmill with an empty cage! I've seen some used with a coonskin cap in the cage. Others used plastic bottles that would rattle around in the cage with results just as effective as a live animal.

Although there used to be a prejudice against swimming, some dog men are currently utilizing it in a keep with good results. The trainer simply walks along the edge of a dock with the dog in the water. When they get to the end of the dock, they simply reverse their field and do this over and over. A variation here is to put the dog in the water, secure the rope from his harness to a stationary underwater two-by-four and then utilize a dog on shore as "bait". The dog will swim mightily in place for an hour or more. Again, of course, the dog must suspect that he will never get to his adversary, but the sight of him there fuels his efforts.

A very common piece of equipment that is used in nearly all keeps is the flirtpole. This is simply a pole, not unlike a fishing pole, with a lure (*i.e.*, a hide) at the end. The trainer runs the lure along the ground and the dog chases it. Usually

Left: A Bulldog loves exercise, and when others are working the mill, he becomes impatient! This is Hammonds' Brainstorm. **Below:** Greenwood's Davis (originally owned by Don Maloney) is a favorite dog of Ralph Greenwood—and for good reason!

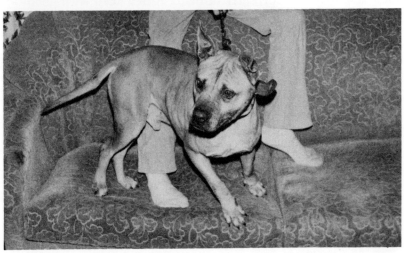

the dog is occasionally allowed to catch and worry the hide (or whatever the lure happens to be). Then the chase is on again!

Whatever method (or combination of methods) of exercise is used-and I have not mentioned them all by any means-after the work period is over the dog is rubbed down thoroughly and weighed. In some keeps the dog is only worked once a day, but in many he is worked twice a day, rubbed down twice, weighed twice and possibly fed twice a day. A typical keep might entail roadwork in the morning and perhaps mill work in the afternoon. Again the method of work is not so important as is the way it is practiced. Most trainers carefully "staircase" the work up, gradually increasing it each day. Some scientific-minded trainers use a hard work day followed by an easy work day that is followed by a still harder work day. This is the "work-recovery" system and the dog is less likely to go stale according to its adherents. Of course the work is still being staircased up but in a slightly different way, and all systems stipulate occasional rest days. In most keeps there is a gradual decrease of work the week before the fight and most have a 48-hour period of no work at all immediately preceding the match. This is so the body will be super-saturated with energy (and the muscles with glycogen) for the match.

A key element of success is carefully coordinating the diet with the work and the weight of the dog. No keep will work well if the trainer is not flexible and so sensitively attuned to his dog that he can sense when a change is needed—and what that change should be! As you can see, a pit dog man has to be fanatically dedicated. He will be practically living with his dog for two or three months. By the time they get to the pit, a dog fighter will know every aspect of his dog far better than any pet owner knows his dog. Our dog man, therefore, is not likely to leave his dog down to be killed.

While it is not part of the keep, an important element of care for the dog is care after the battle. Such care may in-

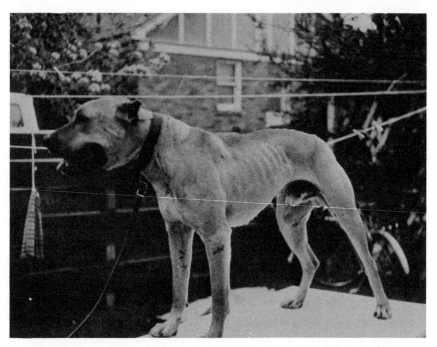

This is Greenwood's Strider at pit weight or possibly below it. Some trainers do not like to draw dogs quite this fine, but it is perfectly possible the dog was below pit weight, then built back up to it, as that is common practice.

volve monitoring the dog's temperature (using hot or cold compresses as needed) and keeping it stable, getting fluid into the animal via an intravenous feeding and in general all around intensive care for several days. Usually the dogs don't need such intensive treatment, but I know of trainers so fanatical that they always apply such therapy as a precautionary action, even when the dog shows no sign of shock. Some dog men are so dedicated that they have paid veterinarians a handsome fee to teach them appropriate techniques. Of course the ideal situation is to get the dog to a veterinarian. But here the loonies have struck again! In several states they have pushed for laws requiring a veterinarian to report any person he suspects has fought his dog. Now there is a piece of truly asinine legislation. The intent, I presume, was to crack down on dogfighting. The effect, quite simply, is that a whole lot of dogs miss out on professional treatment they might otherwise have received, and, because of this, undoubtedly, many lives have been lost that could have been saved.

United States Marines Corporal Dogg performing a climbing feat during a show he was featured in for retarded and handicapped children.

Chapter 10

The Arena

I have never been able to understand why pigeon-shooting at Hurlington should be refined and polite, while a rat-killing match in Whitechapel is low.

T.H. Huxley

In this chapter an actual match scene will be described, but before we get to that I would like to discuss some items that will help put the visions to come into perspective.

I have often been bewildered by the Humane Society's intransigent stand against dogfighting. It isn't just that it is against it; I would expect that, since everyone automatically thinks that fighting is cruel. The only argument, however, I have ever heard made to pit dog men is, "No one would ever say dogfighting was not cruel if they could see the condition of the dogs after a contest." Well, that's like judging the game of football by the battered athletes in the training room! At this point I can hear another cliche mouthed by the humaniacs: "Don't ever compare dogfighting with football. The difference is that the football player is there because he *chooses* to be there. The dog does not." Well, let us put aside the ignorance of philosophical determinism and of human psychology that is manifest in that statement. Instead of getting into technicalities, we will treat the statement as if there were no controversy about the first part of it and take it as it is. Hypothetically let us take the very best football player

Girley Crum's Jake (at left) resents the attention given to a son of Cremator.

that is the most enthusiastic about his sport of any player in the world. Okay? Now multiply his love for the sport by at least a thousand times and we begin to get an idea of just how much a Bulldog loves fighting contact. Incredible? Not really. Simply take into account that a superb human athlete is an accidental combination of genes, whereas the Bulldog is the product of centuries of selective breeding. Well anyway, getting back to the condition of the dogs after a fight, I have always said that the only possible grounds for a charge of cruelty would be the recuperative period afterwards. That, however, doesn't mean that the dogs didn't enjoy the actual fighting. (Otherwise we could argue that the pains of child-birth disprove the joys of sex!) Anyway, the dogs don't really seem to suffer much during recuperation, other than a little soreness and stiffness. The very wounds (the cuts) that bother the critics the most seem to bother the dogs least.

Even granting that there is an element of cruelty to dogfighting, I am puzzled by the priorities of the humaniacs. Why does dogfighting always seem to be the number one target? I have tried to see things through their eyes. It may be that even humane-oriented groups are aware that such things as simple neglect and steel-jawed traps constitute genuine cruelty. It is, however, quite possible that they figure that extenuating circumstances are quite often present in the first case and that trapping is at least of some economic benefit to mankind. With dogfighting, on the other hand, it may seem that there is no excuse for such *premeditated* cruelty. (You can see that I really *am* trying to see things from their perspective!)

I am inclined to think that the real reason behind the order of priorities, though, is a simple matter of the resistance that is met and the support that can be generated. For example, in at least two states proposed felony legislation against animal fighting had included cockfighting. In both cases the cockfighting part of the legislation got kicked off. Why? Well, probably there were at least two main reasons. First, since very few people keep chickens as pets, it was undoubtedly difficult to get people worked up to a feverish-pitch over any sport involving them. Second, chicken fighting is much more widespread than dogfighting. There is considerable money and influence involved. Hence its practitioners were able to make their power felt and quash the section against cockfighting.

It is a significant problem that people have a tendency to think of pit dogs in terms of their pet house dogs. This is a big mistake (unless their house dog is a Pit Bull). A fight would be a very unpleasant thing for their house dog; ergo, it must be unpleasant for a pit dog. The public could stand to be educated about the ways of performance breeds and their owners. For example, the very worst thing you could do to a coonhound would be to make a house dog out of him and never let him hunt! Conversely, it would be cruel to dump

Anderson's Red Baron won over the great champion Fred T in over three hours. Fred T is a very old dog now but still siring pups, and many of them have become champions themselves.

your Bichon Frise in the woods in the dark of night, alone and terrified. The situation is the same, but the choice of breeds makes the difference between misery and pure joy. That's true in dogfighting, too, and it's time our friends learned this simple fact!

There is a qualitative difference in attitude between individual pet owners and the person who thinks of dogs as breeding stock. A famous axiom among show dog breeders is "He who will not drown must not breed." Thus some show dog people drown puppies at birth because they have an obvious fault (*i.e.*, wrong color). I have also known of show dog people who had grown dogs "put to sleep" because they were taking up kennel space that could be used for maturing young dogs that had better conformation. There is nothing cruel in this, of course, but the point is that people who raise dogs generally become less sentimental about the individual dogs and think more in terms of breeding goals. Breeders of performance dogs are even more calloused. It is common practice for bird dog breeders to do their thinning out just prior to hunting season. Those dogs that do not point or are inadequate in other ways are not brought back from the field, but rather they are "planted" there. Dr. Leon Whitney used to claim that the worthiness of a breed was directly proportional to the hard-to-please nature of its breeders. I think he had a point. It is not my purpose to apologize for dog breeders as a group, but I wanted the pit dog men's actions to be judged against that group and not against the individual pet owner. Well, I promised a peek at the pit so here we go.

The site for the matches is the basement of a nearly-completed luxury house. Only the exterior and a few appointments are unfinished. As it turns out the promoter of these matches is a contractor and this is his house and pro-

A scene in a Canadian pit with a little dog that won five and lost two (thus, giving the lie to the humaniac's cry that matches are "to the death").

Nogueira's Patches, a great bitch, won two and lost one. Here she is shown in pit condition.

perty out in the country area of a western state. The eventual buyer of the home will never know what went on one night in his newly prized acquisition. A spiral staircase leads down to the enormous basement. Spotlighted there is a sixteen foot square pit surrounded by three tiers of bleachers. The pit looks something like a boxing ring except that it has wooden sides. The floor of the pit is covered with a red carpet. "Scratch lines" have been laid down in the form of plastic tape four feet out from two of the corners. There is a separate room for weighing and washing the dogs. There is a set of scales and two tubs in the room, one for washing and one for rinsing. A coin is tossed and the winner of the call announces his dog will be washed second. This is to be expected, as the dog that is washed first may use up some of his precious energy in his excitement at being in the pit while waiting for the other dog. Thus, there is a minute advantage to be washed second.

The first dog brought to the pit is a solid reddish fawn-colored dog (fawn is usually called "red" by Pit Bull people). He looks around in eager anticipation for the other dog and meanwhile his handler tries to keep him as quiet as possible. Already members of the audience are offering bets.

"A hundred on the red dog!"

256

THE WORLD'S LARGEST SELECTION OF PET AND ANIMAL BOOKS

T.F.H. Publications publishes more than 900 books covering many hobby aspects (dogs,

. . . BIRDS . .

. . CATS . . .

. . . ANIMALS . . .

. . . DOGS . .

. . FISH . . .

cats, birds, fish, small animals, etc.), plus books dealing with more purely scientific aspects of the animal world (such as books about fossils, corals, sea shells, whales and octopuses). Whether you are a beginner or an advanced hobbyist you will find exactly what you're looking for among our complete listing of books. For a free catalog fill out the form on the other side of this page and mail it today. All T.F.H. books are recyclable.

Since 1952, *Tropical Fish Hobbyist* has been the source of accurate, up-to-the-minute, and fascinating information on every facet of the aquarium hobby. Join the more than 50,000 devoted readers worldwide who wouldn't miss a single issue.

Return To: *Prices subject to change without notice*

Tropical Fish Hobbyist, P.O. Box 427, Neptune, NJ 07753-0427

YES! Please enter my subscription to *Tropical Fish Hobbyist*. Payment for the length I've selected is enclosed. U.S. Funds only.

CHECK ONE: ❏ 1 year-$25.00   ❏ 2 years-$40.00   ❏ 3 years-$60.00   ❏ 5 years-$95.00

       12 BIG ISSUES   24 BIG ISSUES   36 BIG ISSUES   60 BIG ISSUES

(Please allow 4-6 weeks for your subscription to start.)

❏ LIFETIME SUBSCRIPTION (max 30 Years)-$395.00

❏ SAMPLE ISSUE-$3.00

❏ GIFT SUBSCRIPTION. Please send a card announcing this gift. I would like the card to read_____

❏ I don't want to subscribe right now, but I'd like to have one of your FREE catalogs listing books about pets. Please send catalog to:

SHIP TO:

Name_____

Street_____Apt. No. _____

City _____ State _____ Zip _____

U.S. Funds Only. Canada and Foreign add $11.00

Charge my: ❏ VISA   ❏ MASTER CHARGE   ❏ PAYMENT ENCLOSED

_____

Card Number   Expiration Date

Cardholder's Name (if different from "Ship to:")

Cardholder's Address (if different from "Ship to:")

                                        Cardholder's Signature

"You're covered."

"Okay. Who else likes that spotted dog?"

And so it goes. Strange as it may seem, although these bets are strictly verbal, I've yet to see any altercation about someone not paying off.

Now here comes the red brindle-spotted dog carried in the arms of his handler. The dogs are silent but look at each other with the eagerness of two long-lost lovers that can't wait to be in each other's embrace! The referee, a big man with a booming voice, announces the contestants, their weight, 48 pounds, then says, "Ready, gentlemen? Release your dogs!"

The two dogs come together like a couple of freight trains. The red dog immediately takes command, putting the spotted dog down, digging deep into the shoulder and clamping down hard. Neither dog is growling or crying out. The only sound emanating from the pit is the heavy breathing of the dogs and the occasional snapping sound of muscles and tendons under stress. The red dog continues to dominate and he demonstrates that he is a hard biter; he is able to do much more damage than the average dog. The white head and chest of the spotted dog are colored red now, but there is no spurting of blood as a neophyte might expect. At the twenty minute mark the spotted dog begins to even things out. The red dog has not paced himself well and he is beginning to tire. The white dog gets the red dog down now and shakes him with vigor! So goes the fight, with the spotted dog taking over more and more. The red dog occasionally gets the upper hand, but his holds have less authority now. The crushing power in his jaws has ebbed considerably. In the meantime the spotted dog, if anything, seems to be growing in strength. When he has the upper hand, he shakes the red dog until he rattles! Suddenly the red dog turns his head and shoulder away from his opponent but then turns back into him and seizes hold of his lower jaw. It was as though he momentarily lost his enthusiasm for combat and in the midst

The windup to the Smilin' Jack vs Thunder match, with Thunder working over a helpless down and out dog. But mark the amazing sequel. George Saddler saved Jack (the losing dog) and retired him to stud in his kennels. This was a classic match because two great dogs met. Thunder came from behind to win, and Jack never gave up.

of an attempt to escape (or turn away from punishment), he suddenly regained his desire. The handler of the spotted dog asks for a "turn" and the referee obliges, declaring that the red dog has turned. The significance of the turn is that the dogs may now be picked up when they are free of holds and the red dog must demonstrate his willingness to continue the combat by making a "scratch". It is ten more minutes before the handlers are able to pick up the dogs. The red dog holds the lower jaw for three minutes. The spotted dog finally frees himself by pushing into his opponent, twisting and finally getting a nose hold. He throws the dog hard, using the nose hold for some sharp leverage. He shakes the nose hold out and loses it. Quickly he grabs an ear and shakes the red dog hard, banging his head on the padded floor. Finally he lets up a little, standing and resting while holding the red dog's ear. After a brief rest the spotted dog starts to shake the red dog by the ear again and loses his hold. His handler immediately grabs him up in his arms and the other handler deftly picks up the other dog. The dogs are taken to their corners. The referee throws a wet sponge to each dog's handler. The dogs' heads and shoulders are faced to their respective corners, but both are trying to get around to their opponent's. The handlers, meanwhile, are busily checking their dogs' mouths, sponging the dogs down and massaging them. The referee's voice comes booming out. "Twenty-five seconds! Face your dogs! Red dog to go. Ready?" The referee looks at his watch. After five more seconds he commands, "Release your dog!"

The red dog's handler releases his dog and he starts across at a run, headed for his opponent in a line so straight that he might as well be on rails. The spotted dog's handler holds onto his dog until the red dog is nearly there; then he releases him so that he won't bear the full brunt of the red dog's charge. In another two minutes the dogs are momentarily free of holds and are snatched up expertly by their handlers. "Good handle!" compliments the referee. The dogs again are taken to their corners and ministered to as before.

This time it is the spotted dog's turn to scratch. The referee announces, "Twenty-five seconds. Face your dogs!" The handlers swing around. "The spotted dog's turn to go. Stay back of your scratch lines, gentlemen. Ready? Release your dog."

The spotted dog shoots across the pit like a rocket, knocking the red dog into his own corner with the force of his impact! The crowd applauds the spectacular scratch. In another five minutes the dogs are picked up free of holds once again. After the usual ministrations in their corners, the red dog is ordered released for his scratch. The red dog goes across in a rush but stops about six inches from his opponent. The referee begins counting as does a boxing referee after a knockdown. When the red dog fails to take hold by the count of ten, the referee points to the spotted dog's corner and announces him the winner and the time, fifty-five minutes. The handlers leave with their dogs and the bets are paid off among the crowd. Then more dogs are weighed and washed.

There are a total of six matches. Our next match involves two black dogs, one stocky solid-black dog and the other a more rangy dog with a white blaze and white on his chest. At one hour and five minutes the solid black dog's owner concedes the match. Both dogs make game scratches. We see a number of outstanding dogs in the course of the evening. The dogs are cheered alternately by the crowd when they make good scratches or clever maneuvers.

The final match involves two 31-pound females. One of them, Odessa, has won two matches previously, completely devastating opponents in a matter of minutes. Odessa is a good-looking red, red-nosed dog with full drop natural ears. She has a stocky build for a female. The other female is colored identical to Odessa, including exact coat shade and the red nose, but she is rangier and has cropped ears. Her owner has seen Odessa's two prior matches and knows what he is going up against. Obviously he has confidence in his dog's ability.

The match turns out to be a real slugfest. Odessa is not able to dominate this little female as she did the others. In fact, she has her hands full just trying to stay even in this match. Both animals are lightning quick and are expert on attack and defense. First one takes the advantage and then the other. At the hour mark the pace slows. There has not been a turn and there have been no pickups and no scratches. It boils down to gameness now and Odessa is still slightly behind in the match, but she keeps pressing, not allowing her opponent a moment's respite. Finally at an hour and twenty minutes, a turn is called on Odessa. She was not turning away from punishment or because of waning enthusiasm. Rather she made a clever maneuver to escape a hold and gain one for herself, but it is still technically a turn. Odessa scratches "hard and true" as pit dog men like to say, but when it is the crop-eared dog's turn, she stands on her scratch line and takes the count. So Odessa wins in one hour and thirty-seven minutes.

With the sixth match over, let's have a quick critique. First, no dogs were killed in the pit. And no dogs died after the matches. Two dogs were put down afterwards by their owners because they were unsuitable for matching or breeding since they had demonstrated a lack of deep gameness (the loser in the first and last matches). That doesn't mean that there are not matches where a dog dies afterwards; however, it is not the object of the game. Therefore, a sensationalist-type article on pit fighting (written by someone who had obviously never seen one) titled "To the Death" has obviously missed the mark in more ways than one. Especially since an actual death in the pit is a real rarity for several reasons. First, a Bulldog, while formidable, is also tough and hard to kill. Second, the rules provide that a dog loses and the match ends whenever a dog wishes to discontinue the contest. Third, most dog men do have a feeling for their dogs and they are not going to leave them in to be killed for no reason.

Reddick and Beene's Champion Jesse, a littermate to Smith and the great Grand Champion Hank.

Chapter 11

Red Sky in the Morning

Petty laws breed great crimes.

Ouida

He who loves the law and sausages should watch neither being made.

Otto von Bismark

Early one morning in the summer of 1974, I was on my way to a meeting in the north county of San Diego. As I headed up the gigantic ramp to where Highway 805 spans Mission Valley I glanced back to the east and saw a rare phenomenon in our part of the country. A spectacular cherry-red sunrise glowed in the cumulus clouds that towered above the mountains. At almost the same time the radio caught my attention. Washington columnist Jack Anderson was giving his usual early-morning report. As was his custom he ended his broadcast with a series of predictions. In an ominous tone he predicted that the next big scandal would be the cooperation of law enforcement agencies in the staging of "illegal dogfights." Well, if Anderson reported that, I knew that someone was raising Cain in high places about dogfighting. I hated any publicity about pit contests since past experience, although limited, had taught me that in addition to being nonsensical, it nearly always reflected badly on the American Pit Bull Terrier breed. I glanced back at the sunrise again, and I was reminded of an old sailor's proverb: "Red sky at night, Sailors delight; Red sky in the morning, Sailors take warning." I dreaded what was coming.

I did not have long to wait. Soon the papers were filled with all kinds of incredible stories. "Jurors Hunt Police Link in Dogfights" said one headline. "Blood Poured on Dog to Arouse Him for Fight" screamed another. Another stated "Vicious Sport Pits Killer Dogs in Fatal Combat". And so they went, one headline after another, but beneath them all the stories had a definite similarity, as though the news source were the same even though the stories appeared in various different parts of the country. Basically the stories told of how killer dogs were trained for fighting by baiting them with puppies and kittens when they were young. According to the news stories a single fighting dog would kill about 100 puppies and kittens in the course of its training. Then at the fights pigeons were killed and their blood poured on the dogs to arouse them to fight. In spite of all this training the dogs still had to be goaded into fighting by the use of electric cattle prods. Most of the fights ended in death and in forty percent of them both dogs died! Besides the blood and gore there was a definite emphasis on the big money that changed hands at the fights. In addition the matches were a magnet for large scale prostitution and a major market for hard drugs. The point was made that men did these unspeakable things because big money was involved.

Most of the stories emanated from various humane-oriented groups who were in close contact with each other and apparently engaged in a contest to come up with the biggest fairy tale. All of these stories were told without any documentation whatsoever by sources variously cited as "humane officers" or "undercover investigators". One man, in particular, was a purveyor of this type of nonsense and he even started an organization that solicited contributions for fighting this "so-called sport". I don't know how much money was taken in, but I did notice that the individual men-

264

Riptide Buckboard
(Wallace dog)—without
the block of wood in his
mouth.

tioned seemed to have plenty of time on his hands, always traveled first class and was expensively dressed.

I don't want to imply here that there were no sincere people involved in the battle against pit fighting, but obviously there was at least some profiteering involved. And the fact remains that stories were being promulgated as gospel that were absolutely inane and did not contain even a nucleus of truth. The perpetrators of these yarns had to know they were nothing more than that, wild yarns. The situation got to the point that the devotees of the American Pit Bull Terrier practically flinched every time they picked up a paper in anticipation of what the next slanderous item would be. What everybody feared most was a push for legislation to outlaw the breed. Some of us older fanciers remembered the 1948 column by a nationally syndicated writer. According to the columnist a Florida woman had been killed by a pack of Bull Terriers. He "knew" that Bull Terriers were bred and trained to be killers; ergo, the breed should be eliminated. The best way to eliminate the breed was to make it unlawful to possess it. Although that was a different time, I feared that it would not take much to stimulate similar thinking now. My fears were not all that far off the mark. Unknown to any of us, forces were at work in Sacramento to make keeping an American Pit Bull Terrier in California a hazardous enterprise.

I don't remember exactly how the news filtered down, but eventually dog men were made aware of legislation pending in the State Assembly to make dogfighting a felony. By the time I heard about it, some dog men had already made an abortive attempt to stop the bill. A local attorney who was also a Pit Bulldog enthusiast suggested we consult another attorney in town who had been involved in politics and was familiar with the nature of the writhings and slitherings within the catacombs of the state capitol.

At this stage of our story we need to pause for a moment to examine the character of the man who ended up orchestrating the fight against the pending legislation. As a long time resident of San Diego he has accumulated considerable wealth, is quite intelligent and manifests wit and charm; however, he is flawed with a few eccentricities. At one time our crusader was an alcoholic and a hobo. I think it was from those old days that he drew the name for his strain of dogs. In any case some of the old attitudes stuck with him even after he had conquered his alcoholism and became quite successful financially. For one thing he never lost his love for the con and the hustle of his old more poverty-stricken days. He also retained a habit of analyzing everyone and anyone from a strictly cynical point of view. Since I've known him, he has always utilized an adversary system in his business dealings and makes it a point to keep his "adversaries" off balance and on the defense. He hires and fires so many attorneys in his various legal transactions that he has a form letter for doing both. And this was the man who summoned the politically oriented attorney to his home.

The presentation apparently impressed the attorney, for he became convinced of the righteousness of the cause and advised him on how to proceed. He should form an association with the express purpose of fighting the bill. This was done and Morrie Rootberg was made treasurer. The attorney suggested a lobbyist to be utilized who was very close to the governor. Finally he made out a little epistle to be delivered to the legislators. This is what it said:

RE: A.B. 614
        Author: Hon. Mike Antonovich, 41st A.D.
FROM: Association for the Preservation of a Breed
RE: WHY THIS BILL SHOULD NOT PASS

INDEX

  I. *Basic Provisions, A.B. 614*

        This Bill, if passed, would create yet another set of felonies where presently misdemeanor penalties exist . . . with maximum penalties of a $50,000.00 fine, a year and a day in custody, or both.

        The Bill prohibits owning, possessing, keeping or training dogs, with intent that such dog shall be engaged in an exhibition of fighting with another dog, causing one dog to fight another, abetting such activities or allowing them to occur on premises.

Anybody *present* during such activities shall be committing a misdemeanor.

II. *Interested Groups:*
  A. Proponents:
    1. American Dog Owners Association.
    2. One Duncan Wright, Ex-Director of the above.
  B. Opponents:
    1. Association for the Preservation of a Breed.

III. *Arguments Against the Bill:*
  A. *An entire breed of dogs will be endangered if this Bill passes.*
    1. See attached letters from experts in genetics and veterinary science.
    2. *Testing* of any domestic species (thoroughbreds, corn, draft oxen, whatever) are a valid and necessary way to responsibly breed that species.
        Here, the qualities bred for are: intelligence, total compatibility for living within a human family, and courage (in our terms, "gameness").
    3. This Bill is aimed solely at the breeding, training and fighting of a single breed, the American Pit Bull Terrier, the only breed of dogs bred for courage, among other things.
    4. Every effort is made by breeders and owners of these dogs to care for their health and safety. Rules are strictly followed in contests between these dogs in order to insure such care, and to assist proper breeding (see below).
  B. *The proposed penalties under this Bill are egregious, absurd and inconsistent with the other fabric of the Penal Code.*
      This bill would create yet another felony to enforce (with all that that means in governmental expense).

Other felonies exist to protect human safety, or to protect the citizenry aginst dishonorable acts like theft or fraud: these are offenses against persons or society's fabric ... not against the "moral" sensitivities of a small group who have been given "bad scoop", and/or who become faint when they hear of any vigorous activity.

Assemblyman Sieroty voted against this Bill, voicing such sentiments.

Does California really need yet another expensive felony?

C. *The proponents of A.B. 614 have made the following false allegations, here answered:*
1. *Drugs and prostitution are associated with these dogs.*

We know of not one arrest made in California for drugs or prostitution connected with breeding or fighting American Pit Bull Terriers ... over the past ten (10) years.

In any case, this is irrelevant to this Bill: present law can be effectively used against violators of these felonies.

2. *Organized crime and gambling are involved:*

This is silly. The question here is: where is the money? And where is the opportunity for "middle men"?

We challenge the proponents to produce one California District Attorney who has prosecuted for such activities associated with these dogs.

3. *Fighting these dogs is inhumane in that many animals are killed or maimed annually.*

See attached, detailed rules used by all Pit Bull breeders in the United States today. These rules have been used since 1935, and their *purpose* is to protect the dogs from harm, and to meticulously discover which dog will first discontinue the contest.

Above left: Andre Giroux as a young man with his Ch. Sunday. **Above right:** Ch. Panama Red. **Below:** O.C. and T.S.'s Brindle Boss, a two-time winner shown at perfect pit weight.

Above: Corporal Dogg surveys the terrain from a tree she climbed. She also runs the United States Marines obstacle course, including climbing the ropes. **Left:** Clouse's Kito was the sire of Clouse's Big Boy and other good dogs. **Right:** Bull Dozer, a three-quarter Bruno dog that never weighed over 30 lbs. but pound for pound was one of the greatest bulldogs Gary Hammonds ever owned or bred.

4. *Hundred of dogs are hurt or killed annually.*

Breeders with over thirty (30) years experience report that they have seen only two (2) to four (4) dogs actually die during a contest.

This does not compare unfavorably with human sporting contests, such as boxing, football, rodeos, etc.

The reasons for this low number are the rules, referred to above, and the love and care owners and breeders give their animals, and the responsibility they feel to their animals.

5. *The American Pit Bull Terrier is a "Killer Dog", a danger to the safety of man or beast.*

This is a flat lie. Thousands of Californians own these dogs as household pets. They are too friendly to be good watch dogs, and they only fight when they are attacked or, as we say in the animal world, "challenged".

We know of *zero* instances when these dogs have attacked humans . . . a statement which cannot be said of Dobermans, German Shepherds, and other breeds of dogs which are used as watch dogs.

These dogs, quite simply, are very intelligent, friendly and docile—except when "challenged" by another dog.

6. *The breeders, owners and fighters of these dogs are lowlife, irresponsible, heartless creatures.*

This has been the picture so artfully painted by the proponents. It is just not true; and we believe that what is afoot here is the now common phenomenon of scapegoating.

We again challenge the proponents to produce *proof* of this inflammatory allegation.

7. *Dogs are often killed in training.*

This is untrue. It is impossible to kill these dogs in training. Training consists of conditioning which, in many ways, is similar to the conditioning of any other breed of working dog, to wit, work on treadmills, walking and exercising the dogs.

8. *Family pets are often stolen and killed as "bait" by these dogs.*

This is not only fictional, but illogical. These allegations have been made in news stories, but this is something that breeders and trainers of the Pit Bull Terrier absolutely would not and do not do. The dog is a fighter, not a killer, and it would be inimical to any responsible training program that was not bred for that purpose.

Why would a race horse trainer train his horse by racing it against an elephant? The same reasoning applies here: there is no reason why one would engage in such unproductive and despicable acts.

IN SUMMARY: THESE ARGUMENTS ARE IRRATIONAL, ILLOGICAL, UNSUBSTANTIATED AND FALSE.

D. *The proponents are the misled, "lengthening shadow" of a single person, one Duncan Wright.*

Mr. Wright (as can be substantiated by newspaper clippings from across the country) has been touring this country, spreading the false and fallacious arguments outlined above, and attracting innocent citizens into his personal organization, the American Dog Owners Association.

We submit that the poor members of this "Association" have been callously duped by Mr. Wright. We sympathize with these people and invite Mr. Wright to send this document with its supporting data to each of his members.

After all, *if* his allegations were true, what citizen in his right mind would oppose efforts (like A.B. 614) to curb such scandals? Unfortunately, for Mr. Wright and his members, the allegations are simply not true.

E. *The government costs of this Bill, if enacted, would be burdensome.*

These are very tight-budget times in California.

Obviously, this Bill will do its part, if it becomes law, to swell the tasks imposed upon Sheriff's Departments, Police, Jails and the Courts.

We do not know how to measure such cost with precision, but we appreciate, as all Legislators must, that every increment adds to the budget, and makes government more and more complicated in its impact on citizens.

We urge that these costs would be unnecessary, as well as utterly irrational, to incur.

If there is crime, current laws can take care of that.

Money is needed for more important matters than are represented here.

IV. *Conclusion.*

A.B. 614 is ill-conceived legislation which embodies bad public policy. Accordingly, it should not be approved.

Its enforcement will be costly, worthy citizens and activities will be prosecuted, and further felonies with terribly heavy penalties will be added to the Penal Code which, in turn, will contribute to the upward spiral of the cost of law enforcement . . . while diverting law enforcement personnel from more vital citizen-protective functions.

None of the arguments of the proponents hold water under scrutiny, while legitimate animal breeding activities will be stopped.

This Bill will actually place an entire breed of dogs itself in jeopardy of destruction.

For all the foregoing reasons it is submitted that A.B. 614 is a bad Bill, and it should not be approved.

DATED: May 21, 1975
Morris Rootberg

I received this letter and suggested only one change. I felt it was essential to be absolutely honest and for that reason I felt that it was a misstatement to say that American Pit Bull Terriers would only fight when challenged. It is true that there are some that are like that, but there are also many that will go through a screen door or the glass of a window in order to get to a dog. In other respects the letter was completely accurate except for the threat of the breed's extinction. It would be a threat if the law were effective; but I didn't think it would be, and I was right.

In the meantime the president and treasurer of the association met with the lobbyist in Sacramento. According to the lobbyist, chances of stopping the bill were slim, as it had already passed the house and the only chance we would have to make an impact on it would be during the hearing held by the Senate Judiciary Committee. There were two things going for us, though, according to the lobbyist. One was that the bill was a very poorly written one and the other was that the co-authors of the bill did not have much stature among their professional colleagues. In the lobbyist's words, "Two of them don't know enough to find their way to the men's room, and the third can find the way all right but he is at a loss as to what to do when he gets there!"

The association president had trouble marshalling support among the dog men, some of whom were distrustful of him, but many had differing ideas about how to oppose the legislation. Most did not want to expose themselves as dog fighters, and many felt the law would be of little consequence to them anyway. To be honest they had a point, as none of them have been bothered to this day. Those of us who were determined to fight the bill were, however, concerned about more than just the dog fighters; we feared for the owners of the American Pit Bull Terrier in general and indeed for the breed itself. To his credit, the head of the association bore the expense of the lobbyist and attorney with very little help. The rest of us chipped in at least a hundred dollars a piece and one fancier, who has kept several Bulldogs for a number of years but has never so much as observed even a roll, contributed over a thousand dollars. One of the main reasons that non-dog fighters were willing to oppose the bill was that the legislation would make possession of dogs with the intent that they be used in a fighting exhibition a felony. Such language was coming dangerously close to outlawing the breed!

The day of the hearing arrived and a handful of us convened in Sacramento. There was my wife and I, three other dog men and one of them had brought his wife. So we had two women and four men to oppose the bill—not exactly a dramatic show of force! If I had been in charge of this counteraction, I believe I would have had strictly pet owners of the breed on hand and no dog fighters. With dog fighters forming the main composition of the group, the illusion was created that the law would actually curtail the activity. The real threat was to the breed and, in retrospect, I think that should have been the substance of our opposition. The lobbyist, however, set us to do a little amateur lobbying and he instructed that the thrust of our opposition should be that "we don't want to be felons" and that we should stress that the law was unreasonable. So for a full day we set about to "button hole" the members of the Judiciary Committee wherever we could find them, sometimes in their offices but usually in the hallways or on the elevators.

Just before the actual hearing the lobbyist carefully organized how our presentation would be made. First, the opposition (actually the proponents of the bill) would speak. When it came our turn, the lobbyist would speak first. By this time I had already lost considerable faith in the lawmaking process. I did not care much for the lobbying activities and I was shocked to discover that not one commitee member had even looked at the draft that had been carefully drawn up by an attorney and delivered to each of them by registered mail.

The author of the bill spoke first, giving all his puerile reasons for authoring such a legislative monstrosity. The effect of the lobbyist's work was shown in some of the hard questioning that was done by some of the members of the committee.

"Can't current law handle these crimes?"

"Why was cockfighting taken off the bill?"

"If this bill became law, a crime against a dog would be elevated to higher importance than a crime against a human!"

Following the author of the bill came a number of people who spoke for the bill, speaking of the horrible cruelties that were involved in the activity, not the least of which was the stealing of people's pets for the use of training fighting dogs. Of course none of these people, including the author of the bill, had ever seen an honest-to-goodness bona fide dogfight, but they were all "experts"!

Then the lobbyist spoke; agreeing that dogfighting was an unsavory activity, he stressed the unreasonable penalties stipulated by the bill. Then it was my turn. I concentrated on the inaccurate information that had been given the legislators by the proponents of the bill and I asked that the legislators ask for some proof when such allegations were made. I then told them about the admirable qualities of the breed. During this part of my talk, I was interrupted in midsentence by one of the committee members.

"You are just wasting our time telling about the breed, Mr. Stratton. As far as I am concerned, you are breeding dogs for fighting and that is sick!"

I felt my face flush red in anger over the rudeness of the interruption and the unfairness of the remark. Whatever quaver may have been in my voice was gone now—my own fighting blood was up! I heard my voice boom over the P.A. system.

"Mr. Chairman, I have been *trying* to make a point. I have said, first, that the members of this committee have been badly misinformed about the nature of dogfighting. This is fact! We can demonstrate it to the committee if you would give us the time. The other point I was trying to make was that we are dealing here with a worthwhile breed. He is good for things besides fighting and that's why I told you about his use as a catch dog and a hunting dog. Just because someone breeds a dog for gameness does not mean that he is breeding him for fighting. Over ninety-eight percent of the people that keep these dogs only want them for pets, but they still want them to be game."

I was chagrined that I had become angered, as we had been cautioned by the lobbyist not to let that happen. However, everybody seemed to feel that my presentation was a success. In fact, one of the dog fighters ever since then has always said that he wished he had a taperecording of the proceedings just because of my talk. Following me to the podium was the wife of one of the pit dog men. She answered questions posed for her by members of the assembly. One of the main things they wanted to know was the amount of money that changed hands during a match. The woman was honest about the average amount bet and how it all took place.

One assemblyman said to the author of the bill, "Why these people are just making bets like crowds do at a football game, and you're trying to make it seem like a major gambling ring!"

Finally it was time for the vote and I was nearly ecstatic when we had apparently won. The votes to kill the bill were in clear majority! My feelings of triumph were punctured by the lobbyist who explained that several members were not present and they would be in to vote later. We would probably not know until the end of the day whether or not we had been successful. By this time the committee had taken up other matters. But sure enough, as we watched, various committee members came in and proceeded to mark their vote on a whole series of bills in the same way that you or I

Brendy, a great daughter of Eli, with pups.

might mark a ballot. You can imagine how much thought was devoted to each bill! At the end of the day the bill had enough votes to clear it out of committee, and the author of the bill clapped his hands in triumph and accepted congratulations from some of his colleagues.

So that's how it was done. What good was it to be given a chance to speak before the committee if absent members could come in and undo all our good work? We might as well have tap-danced in front of the committee for all the good it did us! Naturally we were all disappointed. For all our work and expense we merely received a rather cynical lesson on the nature of the lawmaking process. I didn't know it then, but I was in for some even more extensive and expensive lessons on the nature of law!

Corporal Dogg, who lately gained nation-wide publicity for killing three coyotes, here receives her official honorary "Lance Corporal" rating as the United States Marines' official mascot. A movie is soon to be made about this Pit Bull. Corporal Dogg went after the coyotes as a result of their having killed a Chihuahua pal of hers.

280

Chapter 12

Bulldogs in the Courtroom

One useless man is called a disgrace. Two or more are called a law firm.

John Adams

Some time in December 1977, a man introduced himself to me as Ed Augustine. He had bought a pup from a guy named Thom Waggoner that I knew casually. He wanted to buy a copy of my book and, like so many that visit here, he wanted information on the dogs. I have mixed feelings about dealing with novices in the breed. On the one hand, I want to help them, especially if they are the type that I think would be an asset to the breed; on the other hand, they can be something of a bore to me since I meet so many of them and they pretty much ask the same old questions. I have, however, never turned one away. In this particular case I should have. He happened to be in the employment of the San Diego Humane Society and he was conducting an undercover investigation.

One time Ed showed up with his "wife". Actually she was a member of the district attorney's staff. I was to learn later that both of them were wired and there was a back-up unit parked a couple blocks away receiving their signals. One misstep here and I would have been off to the slammer!

Well, Ed showed up at various and sundry times on a variety of pretexts. One time he wanted advice on treating his pup. He said Thom had given her a shot of combiotics and he wondered if I had anything that would help. In retrospect this was a ludicrous action on his part, as he was deliberately trying to set me up for a charge of practicing veterinary medicine without a license. As a matter of fact, Waggoner was later charged with the offense because he took a dollar from Augustine for the shot of combiotics that he administered. Ed was just spinning his wheels in my case, though, because I never take money for any veterinary services I might render. In this particular case I recommended a veterinarian that I considered quite competent. (Without a doubt, they then proceeded to investigate him for complicity in dogfighting.)

Throughout several months Ed would call and come by for a variety of reasons. I didn't pay too much attention to him, as he was just one of many, so I don't recall a whole lot about the details of the visits. Ed, however, was recording every happening and quoting me directly on a number of occasions in the reports that he made after every visit. I do recall, however, that I showed him a Xerox copy of an advertisement that Howard Heinzl had sent me. The ad was for an oil-drilling tool called the Pit Bull Mud Mixer. Since the advertisement featured a picture of a Pit Bull and referred to the breed, it was of interest to American Pit Bull Terrier fanciers. Heinzl had written on the back of the copy, "If I had my way, they'd have their picture on the dollar bill." Saying that he was a printer, Ed asked if he could take the copy and see if he could get additional copies made. In the middle of the week he called and said he had fifteen copies of that ad for me. I was busy at the time and I had a lot of work to do, so I told him I would call him at a later date. As it turned out there were several people coming over on Saturday. I thought this was a good time to have Ed over too, thus killing several birds with one stone! So I gave him a call and he arrived late after just about everyone else had gone. The only one still present was Jesse Boykin who wanted to buy a dog.

I don't normally sell dogs, but Jesse was interested in the

Tombstone proved to have very deep gameness and ability in his very first match, so he was retired to stud, and has sired a number of outstanding progeny.

same line of dogs as I was and had taken excellent care of a female that he had gotten from me earlier. In trying to decide between two different females, we were trying to get them to work the springpole. One of them, Dolly, was not getting the idea, so I brought out Honeybear, who was a real whiz on the springpole. The idea was that Dolly would be excited by the sight of Honeybear working the springpole and would be inspired to work it herself. For some reason Honeybear, who had been perfectly friendly to Dolly on other occasions, ignored the springpole and scratched straight into Dolly! Well, I was surprised that Dolly would even fight, as she had shown no signs of aggression at all and she was just a young dog. But fight she did, and she had Honeybear by the ear and was really manhandling him. We separated the dogs immediately and returned them to their kennel runs.

Tuesday evening May 9, 1978, at about seven o'clock, I had just settled down to some reading. There was a knock at the front door. When one of my sons answered, the man stated he had an arrest warrant for Richard and Stephanie Stratton. Thinking it was one of my friends trying to be funny, I went to the door and was startled to find several strangers on my doorstep with a *bona fide* arrest warrant. They also had a search warrant and "Captain" Virden, head of the local Humane Society, entered with his entourage. Under his supervision a complete search was made of my premises. They even went through my boys' room with a fine-toothed comb. My eight dogs were carted off in Humane Society trucks. Pictures were taken of them and their names were stamped on their collars. Then I remembered. Only a few days earlier Ed had asked for detailed specifications on kennels for Pit Bulls. At the time I did not realize that I was giving information on how to house my own dogs!

Snakeman's Gator II is an inbred grandson back to three littermates which comprised some of the best known pit dogs in the country namely, Zebo, Vindicator, and Rosie.

Kinard's Mike, taken many years ago at Leo Kinard's country place. (This was a Wallace-bred dog that won several matches for Kinard).

In the meantime a crowd had gathered out front. The lights from the television cameras and a large number of police and Humane Society vehicles were drawing people from all over. The television people tried to interview my neighbors, but they refused to say anything bad about me, so none of that was aired. Captain Virden, however, provided them with an interview, saying that this was the biggest dogfighting bust in fifteen years. When one of the interviewers stated that the dogs were obviously well cared for, Capt. Virden responded that he didn't have much regard for people that lavished all this loving care on an animal only to put in a pit to die. "I don't call that humane," he concluded dramatically, "I call that rotten!" There was no basis whatsoever for that remark. I had never matched any dogs and with the single exception of an accidental kennel fight, I had never had a dog killed fighting; and Virden had no reason to believe that I had. Besides that, Virden had told me that the television people had found their way to my house by monitoring their radio transmissions. Well, that was a lie, as I later found out from the television people that Virden had called them. But that was only the beginning to a whole lot of lying.

At the same time that our place was raided, Waggoner and Boykin were being subjected to the same thing. Poor Jesse had only one dog (his house dog) and they confiscated it. In my case, in addition to my dogs, treadmills, springpoles, breaking sticks, all kinds of correspondence, magazines and books were confiscated. Jesse had none of these things, so they confiscated among other things a broken badminton pole!

While the television cameras came to my house and I received the brunt of the publicity, at least I was not subjected to the degrading treatment that Boykin and Waggoner received. They showed up at Jesse's place of employment and took him away in handcuffs. Waggoner was handcuffed and forced to lie face down while they carted off his dogs and searched his house. In retrospect I am amazed at my calm while my family sat in unbelieving silence. Perhaps I, too, was in a state of shock. I had never been arrested before for anything, and I had just had my driver's license automatically extended because I had received no moving violation over four years' time. Whatever was back of all of this I felt the best immediate course of action was to be cooperative, and I had faith that everything would right itself in the end. In the meantime it hurt me to see dogs that had been raised from puppyhood on my place carted off. My wife was in tears and begged Virden that we be allowed to see the dogs. Virden assured her that she could visit them the next day. Another lie! It was six weeks before we were allowed to see our dogs and that required a court order!

The next day we surveyed the wreckage of our lives, or so it seemed at the time. The newspapers were running front-page headlines on the story. We were receiving crank phone calls and crank mail. In order to get the arrest and search warrants Augustine had sworn out an affidavit saying that I had called him and invited him to a dogfight and that he had witnessed a fight on my property. The papers quoted from the affidavit and then filled in with general information

Girley Crum on the left with a fellow dog enthusiast.

about dogfighting that they apparently got from the Humane Society.

One of the few bright spots in those dark days was the way our friends rallied to our support. I was concerned about the reaction of the other faculty members at school, but I need not have been. They were foursquare behind me, absolutely convinced that I would not be involved in anything wrong, and they all offered to testify for me if it came to that. It was truly heartwarming. I was especially thankful to my mother-in-law, Stella Slosky. It would have been easy for her to have been bitter. Here I had taken her daughter who had been reared in the lap of luxury and not only had I failed to provide her with the things to which she had become accustomed, but I had also gotten her thrown in jail! She and my father-in-law Sam, however, were completely supportive. They helped us out in so many ways that I don't think I ever did thank them properly—until now.

After these events transpired it was time to start looking for an attorney. I had never needed one before in my life, so I had no idea what criteria to utilize in selecting one. Several of my friends are attorneys, but they live out-of-state. One of them suggested that I consult with several, then go with the one with whom I felt most comfortable. After hearing our story, one attorney shook his head. According to him the Humane Society was a tough opponent to go up against in court. They always had the sympathy of the jury and had a built-in aura of respectability. A typical Humane Society case, according to this attorney, went along these lines. An old woman outlives all her friends and has few relatives and little purpose in life. She feeds and adopts a stray cat and then another. The process continues until she has an abundance of adopted cats. Eventually, as she gets older, she is less able to care for her charges. She has barely enough food and can't afford medical bills. A few of the cats develop skin problems and all of them are a trifle underweight, but she is too softhearted and sentimental to have the cats destroyed. So she gets busted by the Humane Society which apparently does not concern itself with the cats running wild that are underfed and have skin problems. This particular attorney, incidentally, considered the Humane Society a blight on society in the sense that it tended to elevate animal concerns way above human considerations.

One of the things I was unprepared for was the competition among lawyers. We consulted several because we felt that we wanted the very best, but we didn't expect them to call back in the evening like car salesmen! After about two weeks we settled upon Charlie Harrod as our attorney. Charlie was bright and engaging and he was the nephew of world-famous attorney Vincent Hallinan. We liked all the attorneys with whom we consulted, but we were especially impressed with Charlie's candor.

In the meantime poor Jesse had to get a loan on his house to afford an attorney, and not a very good attorney at that. At least we didn't think so. His opinion was that we would have no chance in a trial because it would be our word against the law enforcement officer (in our area, humane agents are deputized), and juries rarely believed defendants in such cases. His approach was to try to get a "deal". The deal he negotiated was a reduction to a misdemeanor for Jesse if he would testify against me. This Jesse refused to do, so he decided to get another attorney. He secured the services of Gordon Frevel, Charlie's partner.

One of the things an attorney does is try to negotiate a "deal" through plea bargaining. Forget about the principle of not being guilty we were told. If the case went to trial, there was always the chance of a conviction, guilty or not. An attorney's job is to minimize the amount of possible harm to his client. As it turned out, however, the only deal they would negotiate involved my bringing evidence against Larry McCaw. Virden in his talk to the news media had promised more arrests and although he didn't name anyone, he made reference to a prominent businessman, a college professor and a doctor that were involved in this "ring". I knew the people he was talking about and now it became clear that I was supposed to buy my way out of trouble by turning state's evidence against these people. Specifically they were after McCaw. Even if I had been inclined to go along with this (and I was not), Charlie wouldn't have let me. He was not the type of attorney that believed in getting his client off by "selling out" someone else! Stephanie and I dreaded the trauma of a trial, but we girded ourselves for the inevitable. In the long run we preferred complete absolution of guilt anyway.

An important part of trial is the selection of a jury. The defense is trying to get people that will be sympathetic and the prosecution is trying to get rid of them! So even before the trial begins, the adversary system is in full effect and the battle is joined. Charlie and Gordon wanted our reactions in the selection of a jury, for a gut reaction seemed to be even more important than many years of experience with various juries. There were only two people about whom there was any disagreement. One was the wife of a police officer. Charlie definitely wanted to bump her, as he felt she would be prejudiced in favor of any badge-toting witness, even a Humane Society officer. I, however, was the son of a police officer (in fact, my father had been chief of the campus police at the University of Colorado) and I was not inclined to view the "police mentality" as cynically as was Charlie. Besides, we would have two police officers testifying for our side. In addition, the juror in question had testified that she would not give more weight to a police officer's testimony, and in so saying she laughed and rolled her eyes as though to emphasize that she knew they were no more truthful than anyone else. The other juror in question was a fundamentalist minister. Charlie wanted to bump him on the basis of past experience with fundamentalist-type ministers. In his experience they were too doctrinaire and judgmental and tended to be prosecution-oriented, but I liked him and thought he would be okay.

The jury was selected in two days and the prosecution began its case on the third day. The case very simply was testimony by Augustine who alleged that the accidental fight in my backyard had been purposeful. In addition, my treadmill, springpole, breaking sticks and books were put into evidence. Charlie wasted little time in cross-examination of Augustine and the prosecution rested its case after testimony of the Humane Society veterinarian.

While the prosecution only had three witnesses (Augustine, the agent who executed the search warrant and the veterinarian), the defense compensated with a plethora of witnesses. I led off. Under questioning by Charlie I denied the fight in my backyard had been purposeful and I explained that the purpose of the springpole was for the enjoyment of the dogs. Then came a variety of witnesses. John Gray from the Los Angeles Police Department testified that he kept Pit Bulls and that breaking sticks were a necessity. He also testified that my reputation among dog people was that I did not fight dogs. Pretty much the same thing was testified to by Al Stone, a retired police officer and now an attorney. Tom Stoneburner and Brad Powell of the Golden State Pit Bull Club also testified along similar lines. All of these people made outstanding witnesses, but one of the most outstanding was Suzie Stewart, an admitted out-of-state dog fighter. My attorney claimed she was the best witness he had ever had in all his years of law practice. Beautiful, radiant and articulate, Suzie testified that she and her husband had agreed to sell me an outstanding dog named Dillinger. She explained that no one else would ever have gotten the dog because they would have been tempted to match him, and he was too valuable to utilize for anything other than as a stud dog. Her appearance was so angelic and she was so articulate that she tended to dispel the dog fighter stereotype. And I'll never forget Harriet who testified to my reputation. Under cross-examination, the prosecutor posed a question for her: "If I told you that a Humane Society officer had witnessed Mr. Stratton fight two dogs, would that change your opinion of him?"

"I'm under oath," said Harriet after a thoughtful pause, "and I have to tell the truth." She gave another thoughtful pause and the prosecutor waited with a pleased look on his face. Then she added, "I would have to cast serious doubt as to the reliability of that officer!"

At times the trial seemed downright unreal. The prosecution had brought in all my dogs for the jury to view and he took the incredible position that since my dogs wanted to fight, I had trained them to be that way. (Augustine's testimony implied that you had to train your dogs to fight. He said the one he bought from Waggoner showed no inclination to fight. Of course, it was still basically a pup!) Well, we brought in someone unimpeachable to counter that argument in the personage of Senator Mills. President Pro Tem

Corporal Dogg, like so many Pit Bulls, is quite adept at tree climbing.

of the State Senate, Senator Mills, who had owned four Pit Bulls testified that they did not have to be trained to have the fighting urge. He also said some nice things about the American Pit Bull Terrier which warmed my heart. One of the main things he stressed was the breed's good disposition and unusual tolerance of the maulings of small children. The only drawback about his testimony was that it drew further media attention to the trial.

After all the witnesses came the closing arguments. The prosecutor, ostensibly because the burden of proof is on him, gets to speak twice. To my amazement the prosecutor did not even try to allege that I ever matched a dog. All that he tried to say was that I had rolled my dogs. This brought to mind that one of the authors of the bill had reassured a group of people that the law had been deliberately worded so that it was aimed only at people that were matching dogs. Now here was some hardheaded prosecutor trying to make "every aspect of fighting dogs" (in his own words) a felony. Again, this was dangerously close to outlawing the breed.

Then came the long wait after the case went to the jury. It was a long wait too. For several days we waited. When the jury finally came in, it was to report that they were hopelessly deadlocked on Stephanie and me; however, they did acquit Jess. As we learned later the very people that I was adamant about leaving on the jury, the fundamentalist minister and the policeman's wife, were the ones that held out for conviction! So much for my intuition regarding jurors!

The trial had lasted two weeks. It had been long and expensive for the state, and since the jury had been hung in favor of acquittal, conventional wisdom held that the case would be dismissed. A telephone call from Charlie brought bad news. We were going back to trial!

Caleb Douglas and Thunder, the Schutzhund dog.

Chapter 13

Triumph and Tragedy

Wise men argue causes, and fools decide them.
                                    Anarchus

Before we went to trial the first time, we had been told that the percentages are in favor of the prosecution. Now we were informed that the prosecution wins an even higher percentage of retrials. (If they aren't sure they are going to win, they don't take the case back!) Ironically we had drawn a "bulldog" of a prosecutor and he was "scratching" right back into us!

With the percentages weighed in favor of the prosecution, we decided to take on an additional attorney. We had seen Matt Lees at work at a preliminary hearing and we were impressed by him. Our confidence had not been shaken in Charlie—far from it!—but we were determined to win, redeem our reputations and save the lives of our dogs.

From what I've said before, the reader may have gathered that I have lost some of my former respect for lawyers and judges generally. The reader would be right! I never realized before what a collection of drunks comprised the law profession! "Sober as a judge" lost considerable impact when I watched many of them stagger out of the bar called "The Gavel" across from the courthouse. However, my respect for certain individual jurists was tremendous. I had considerable admiration for our first judge, but I was to gain even greater admiration for the judge that presided over the second trial.

Hubbard's Big Boy, a son of Clouse's Kito, was a great 44-pound dog that won several matches.

His name was Norbert Ehrenfreund and he was unbelievably diligent in his duties. He kept a tight rein on the prosecution *and* the defense, while being fair to both. In addition he was considerate and compassionate.

One incident will illustrate the compassion of the judge. During the course of the trial we maintained our habit of visiting our dogs weekly. Of course, as I mentioned earlier, it was six weeks before we were able to begin seeing our dogs and it took a court order for that! (In fairness to the Humane Society, they had what they thought was a good reason for denying us access. In two previous cases where pit dogs had been confiscated in the state, the dogs were broken out of the kennels. With these facts in mind, two armed deputies from the sheriff's office were assigned to guard the premises around the clock.) I'll never forget our shock at the sight of our dogs on our very first visit. Three of them were so skinny that you could all but see through them. To compensate for that three others were so obese they could hardly walk. I was absolutely astounded that the dogs would be allowed to get into such a condition. Couldn't these people see? Both of us were quite upset over the condition of our dogs; however, Humane Society officials were very cooperative in acceding to our requests on how the dogs were fed. They were quite willing to give our dogs special treatment, probably because they thought we would end up paying for it anyway!

A change in attitude occurred after the first trial. Even after his acquittal Jess had to obtain a court order for the release of his dog. To Jesse's amazement, the prosecutor asked that the Humane Society be reimbursed for boarding Boykin's dog. The judge, of course, would have none of that, saying that making an acquitted person pay for that would be a little "harsh", like making an innocent man have to pay room and board for the time he had spent in jail! For whatever reason, after the first trial things started to go downhill again. During the final week of the second trial we were dismayed to find one of our dogs, "Star", so weak she could hardly walk. Sgt. Crawford, who was overseeing our visit, agreed that the dog was in bad shape and referred her case to the veterinarian that tended the dogs at the Humane Society. We weren't satisfied with her progress and our attorney asked the judge that this one dog be released to our custody for personalized attention. As always, the prosecutor saw some dark plot in this and nearly had a hemorrhage that something might go our way. Here is my point. It would have been easy for the judge to have shrugged the whole thing off. After all, the dog was under the care of the veterinarian and in the custody of the Humane Society which (to give them their just due) has developed an apparently unassailable reputation. However, this judge convened the court (without the jury) at the Humane Society kennels and had their veterinarian explain the dog's condition. He then ordered that the dog be sent to an independent veterinarian for a blood scan and recommendations.

The point of all this is that the compassion, efficiency and plain human decency of certain jurists, like Judge Ehrenfreund, and even of some of the lawyers, commanded my admiration and tended to offset my initial negative impression of the entire judicial system.

The second trial went pretty much like the first except that it lasted longer. For some reason the prosecutor took an entire week to select a jury. Perhaps he felt it was the jury's fault that he lost the first time. Another major change was that not only did the prosecutor not bring the dogs in, but he also fought tooth and nail against our request to have them brought in. Obviously he realized that the charm of these dogs had had some sort of effect on the previous jury. We were allowed to bring in only one dog, Honeybear, and that was because there had been considerable testimony about that specific dog introduced by the prosecutor. He was my only scarred dog, but we had accounted for the scars. I was on the stand when Honeybear was brought in. As before I could tell that the charm of the dog was having an effect. Matt showed Honeybear to the jury and demonstrated his friendliness toward humans, but the prosecutor demanded to know what would happen if another dog were present. I answered honestly, "He would attack with abandon. But there would be no hatred in it, just a joyous love of battle."

Well, anyway, the case finally went to the jury. They quickly came back with a not-guilty verdict and our long nightmare was finally over. Our dogs had been in custody since May 9th, and we were acquitted on December 22nd. Some of our friends felt that we should force the Humane Society to deliver our dogs to us since the law specifically provided for that. In the glow of victory, however, I had no desire to rub the society's nose in what they had done. There were occasions on which society personnel had been very considerate of us and we had actually grown to like some of them.

In any case I held no hatred for the Humane Society, but I still despised that stupid law! At the beginning of the ordeal when we were shopping for an attorney, several of them looked the law up and shook their heads. Here is how it reads:

PENAL CODE 597.5 Dog Fights-Training, Conducting, Attending.

(a) Any person who does any of the following is guilty of a felony and is punishable by imprisonment in a state prison not to exceed one year and one day, or by imprisonment in a county jail not to exceed one year, or by a fine not to exceed fifty thousand dollars ($50,000), or by both such fine and imprisonment:

(1) Owns, possesses, keeps, or trains any dog, with the intent that such dog shall be engaged in an exhibition of fighting with another dog.

(2) For amusement or gain, causes any dog to fight with another dog, or causes any dogs to injure each other.

(3) Permits any act in violation of paragraph (1) or (2) to be done on any premises under his charge or control, or aids or abets any such act.

(b) Any person who is knowingly present as a spectator, at any place, building, or tenement where preparations are being made for an exhibition of the fighting of dogs, with the intent to be present at such preparations, or is knowingly present at such exhibition or at any other fighting or injuring as described in paragraph (2) of subdivision (a), with the intent to be present at such exhibition, fighting or injuring is guilty of a misdemeanor.

"A catch-all law" is how one attorney described it. "It really gives broad authority to the loonies!" said another. My main objection to it all along, of course, was that innocent owners of the American Pit Bull Terrier might be harrassed or arrested. Little did I ever think, though, that I would end up being the victim of it. I was so busy worrying about others that I forgot to cover my own *gluteus maximus*.

Shortly after my trial I was asked by some dog men in Arizona to speak to the state assembly committee there, as they, too, were considering a law worded nearly identical to the abomination that had been passed in California. This whole thing had been instigated by Augustine who testified before an assembly committee there to the effect, apparently, that California had a very fine law that was driving all the dog fighters out of California and over to Arizona. The obvious implication was that Arizona needed a similar law.

I testified that (1) pit dog men were not leaving California *en masse*, (2) there were undoubtedly more fights held in California than in Arizona, and (3) innocent people could be harrassed. I also gave an account of my recent experience. After hearing all this, all one legislator could think to ask was, "Do you presently live in Arizona, Mr. Stratton?" When I said that I didn't, he wanted to know why I was over there poking my nose in Arizona's affiars. It didn't matter, apparently, that Augustine also was from out-of-state! When I replied that I was concerned about the breed and its owners regardless of location, he asked, "Well, are you going to go to all the other states to testify, too, if they want to pass a law?" This turkey was simply being obnoxious! There was no point to his questions.

"Senator," I replied, "it is my fervent hope that any other state legislators will have the sagacity not even to consider such egregious legislation!"

I knew from the start that there was no stopping the steamroller. There were several television crews present and with all the media coverage there was just no way that those political animals were going to fail to pass that legislation and be known as a "pro-dog-fighter"! A couple of the legislators spoke apologetically to me in private afterwards. One said she would try to have the bill killed in the assembly. Another vowed to take the teeth out of it. It, however, never happened and I never thought it would.

Another person speaking apologetically to me was the S.P.C.A. director. He told me that he knew the inside story on my case and he was well aware of what a miscarriage of justice it was that I was even charged in the first place. "Well, then," I asked, "why did you support the very legislation that made it all possible?"

"Well, we just felt we had to put an end to all this dogfighting."

At that point I gave up. I had just finished testifying as to the ineffectiveness of the law in California!

During the course of the hearing these legislators, too, made assurances that this law would not be used against someone who merely game tested his stock! Now where did I hear that before?

Meanwhile, the Waggoner trial had ended with a conviction. Much to the dismay of the prosecutor at sentencing, the judge reduced Waggoner's conviction to a misdemeanor and gave him a suspended sentence. The prosecutor protested that such leniency would not provide a deterrent for other dog fighters. The judge dismissed that idea contemptuously saying that they were never going to get dogfighting stopped. Well, then, the prosecutor wanted Waggoner to pay the board bill for his dogs—a mere $18,000! This, too, the judge refused to grant, saying that it was not Waggoner's idea that the dogs be kept there; in fact, he had asked for their release and the prosecution insisted that they were evidence. Then, obviously feeling the sting of defeat, the prosecution asked for a court order to destroy the dogs. This the judge did grant and I am told that both Augustine and the prosecutor smiled for the first time that day. These agents of the Humane Society were now showing their true colors!

Matt Lees was the defense attorney for Waggoner too and he beseeched the judge for a stay on the order to destroy the dogs. Saying that he did not want to destroy the dogs, the judge granted the stay. The judge had asked for an alternative, so Matt went to work. He got a dog trainer to evaluate the dogs' suitability as pets. The prosecutor then insisted that they be allowed to send their trainer too! Their representative had been a former member of the board of directors for the Humane Society and his wife was still on the board, so you can imagine his objectivity! It turned out that the defense advised adoption and the prosecution's witness advised that they all be destroyed. The judge finally caved in and ordered the destruction of the dogs. This was in the face of the fact that Matt had obtained a hundred names of people who would not only give the dogs a home but would submit to periodic inspection by the Humane Society. The prosecution, however, had come in armed with letters from other humane societies, saying that Pit Bulls have been involved in attacks on people. (I can't think of any breed that hasn't.) Three Pekingese were reported to have killed a baby a few years back. Naturally, some breeds are more likely to attack than others, but neither the Pit Bull nor the Staf appear on the list of breeds that are problem biters. The statement that Pit Bulls were not suitable pets is not even worthy of comment.

The whole affair was capped off by the unseemly haste with which the dogs were destroyed. By the time Matt got word of the order the dogs were already dead and the press was asking for a statement. They got one. Matt appeared on television that night exuding cold fury. You see, Matt had been in to visit the dogs and he knew that there was not one there that was not suitable for adoption. This whole thing was a simple vendetta by the Humane Society. Even the judge had commented about the grudge that the Humane Society seemed to have against these dogs. The ludicrous thing was that many of the dogs had been born and raised right there in the Humane Society kennels, and the Humane Society's haste in destroying the dogs completely circumvented the appeal that, by law, Matt had the right to file within 48 hours of the time the order was issued.

Up to this particular point in time I had always viewed the Humane Society as a basically good organization filled with well-meaning people. Their intentions were good, but they were just a little misguided about dogfighting. However, after all those dogs were killed for no reason other than the

Crenshaw's Black Jack, a son of Crenshaw's Reno and Crenshaw's Smokey (a daughter of Sad Sack).

appeasement of the Humane Society, my attitude changed. How could I have respect for such petty, narrow-minded and vindictive people? I didn't blame the judge because, after all, he didn't know any better. The Humane Society did, however, and I don't think the stink of what they did should ever be allowed to escape them. But for them, eighteen dogs and puppies could be alive right now and living in good homes. I guess I was not the only one that was disgusted. A few months later the local animal control asked that their names be taken off the membership list because "of certain recent events".

All along, spokesmen for the Humane Society had maintained that they were not against the breed; in fact they admired the dogs. It was the people who "misused" them that they were after. In the final analysis, however, the dogs were their victims.

At the present time a petition has been initiated by parties having no connection with Pit Bulldogs to ask that the grand jury investigate certain incidents, including the destruction of the dogs.

PIT BULL
Tough at any weight.

Like a fighting pit bulldog, the new Pit Bull mud agitator from Geosource is rugged, durable, and efficient. Designed and built specifically to withstand the most severe mud mixing conditions, Pit Bull gets tough and stays tough at any mud weight.

Just as the pit bull is bred for strength and tenacity, the Pit Bull was engineered for (not designed around) the heavy mud weights and extreme shock loads which mud mixers are subjected to. Heavy-duty, high efficiency, low-noise helical and spiral bevel gears, oversized shafting, Timken 30,000 Hr. B-10 tapered roller bearings, splash lubrication, easy access to drive internals, interchangeability of sub-assemblies, and pitched blade turbine impeller are some of the outstanding features of the Pit Bull mud agitator.

Extensive preplanning in fluid mechanics and mud composition enables your Geosource representative to supply you with the exact unit for your drilling requirements. Standard Pit Bull models range from 5 to 20 horsepower, with a wide AGMA speed selection from 37 to 100 RPM. Gear boxes are available in three sizes.

Call your Geosource man today and let him show you who's the new boss in mud mixers. Oil Tool Division, Geosource Inc., P.O. Box 9489, Houston, Texas 77011, 713/676-1111, Telex: 775409.

Oil Tool Division
Geosource Inc.

GEOSOURCE

This layout is not atypical of many other advertisements that have begun to feature the Pit Bull. Television commercials are even appearing which utilize the American Pit Bull Terrier to characterize the products being advertised.

304

Chapter 14
The Invincible Bulldog

They can because they think they can.
Virgil

In the pages of this book I have taken pains to give the readers a peek at the world of dogfighting because I think it is important to know at least a little about it in order fully to understand the breed. A knowledge of the real world of dogfighting gives a new perspective for viewing various ideas on the history of the breed and also for evaluating the incredibly imaginative tales disseminated by various propagandists who view dogfighting as mankind's most vile activity. There is, however, more to the American Pit Bull Terrier than fighting ability. The following articles tell about some of his other activites.

CATCH'EM & FETCH'EM
Don Livingston
(*Bloodlines, Journal* May-June 1979)

Since subscribing to *Bloodlines Magazine* beginning about a year ago, I have read many interesting articles, and seen some fine APBT specimens. However, I have yet to read an article concerning what this great breed of dog does instinctively, and incomparably to any breed I know of. So I figured it was time for me to share with *Bloodlines* a little hobby that my APBT "Spike" and I got into a year ago.

Spike is almost five years old now, and he has lived with me since he was a mere five weeks old. The only knowledge I had of the APBT at that time was only what I could manage to find to read which wasn't much more than an encyclopedia. Needless to say, I had quite an education ahead of me, but I guessed that Spike and I would live and learn together.

Spike grew up on St. Simons Island in Southeastern Georgia, where marshland is most prevalent. Inhabiting this marshland, primarily hunted with shotguns or high powered rifles, is what we know as the "wild hog", a very agile, strong, and dangerous game animal. While out driving my car one afternoon, I pulled in behind several fellows in a pick-up truck carrying a dogbox which had in it an APBT, and a large mixed breed bulldog. I noticed them turning off in front of a roadside country store, and curiosity got the best of me so I followed them. As I approached the dogbox, I heard a loud commotion taking place in the truck, obviously coming from an unknown source. I hurried up to the truck to look in and see a tough looking South Georgia Piney Woods Rooter (wild boar hog) laying there hogtied. Immediately I engaged in conversation with these fellows. It was right then and there that I was introduced to the sport of wild hog hunting with the APBT. They explained to me how they caught the wild boar with their two dogs, and that this was a sport they frequently participated in. They went on to tell me that not only was this a very challenging sport, but by catching the hogs alive with the dogs, it enabled them to pen the hog for fattening, and eventual tablefare or to use the hog for marketing purposes.

Being an avid hunter anyway, this idea of hunting and taking alive a very dangerous game animal, with such a courageous breed of dog aroused my interest so that it was just a matter of days before I looked into a reliable source for an APBT puppy.

During this deliberation, I discussed with Dan McCrary (a very close hunting buddy) what I had discovered about this sport involving such a fearless dog. Knowing Dan like I did, his immediate and ecstatic interest in this breed of dog did not surprise me. So just like that, Dan and I were searching for APBT puppies together. After doing some research, we discovered the O.L. Hill APBT farm in San Angelo, Texas, which happened to be very reputable. Within a month's time, Dan and I were in Jacksonville,

Don Livingston's Spike, a wild boar and catch dog *par excellence.*

Florida, picking up our puppies from the Jacksonville Airport.

It was only two months later that I tested Spike's catching instincts on a forty-five pound pig, which we had tied out in the yard on a thirty foot rope. Within seconds this innocent three month old puppy charged in, caught and held the pig by the ear like a veteran with many years experience. I knew right away that I had a natural born "catch dog."

It has been five years since Spike, as a young puppy, caught his first hog in my yard. He has caught many wild hogs in the marshes surrounding St. Simons Island since that time. Over the years as Spike has matured, I have found, not to my surprise however, that wild hogs are not the only animals, wild or domestic, which activate Spike's instincts, which brings us to the title of this article.

A year has passed since Spike and I left St. Simons Island, and moved to the neighboring state of South Carolina. To this date, I have not found any wild hogs for Spike and me to hunt in our new location, although I understand there are some sparsely scattered about in the swamps.

While discussing hog hunting one day with Roy Hudson, a friend and co-worker, he suggested since farming is the primary industry in this area, that I should divert Spike's instinctive abilities toward assisting farmers with stray or runaway livestock. From this suggestion of Roy's came the idea of Catch 'Em and Fetch 'Em, which not only is a sport and hobby to Spike and myself, but also a very helpful and friendly service for local farmers.

Catch 'Em and Fetch 'Em has been in existence now for about one year, and has been a lot of fun for Spike and myself. We have gotten numerous calls from farmers with livestock problems, whether it be strays that take up inhabitance in neighboring swamps in which man cannot get close enough to catch himself, or an ornery old boar hog or bull which refuses to load up at market time. So far Spike's biggest and most exciting catch was a 2600 pound Charlet Bull. It was tough, but Spike got the job done. For some reason a bull, even as large as this, does not like a 65 pound APBT hanging on his tender nose, the results being this massive beast dropping to his knees in surrender; then it's loading time.

All of you who own an APBT already known how competitive this great breed of dog is. Don't be hesitant in letting your APBT demonstrate this competitive spirit and ability, should the situation ever arise, towards a worthy experience such as I have done with Spike.

SCHUTZHUND DOG (PROTECTION DOG)
Ralph Greenwood

(*Pit Bull Gazette,* Volume 1 No. 4)

Just last week, I received a letter that I believe would be of interest to other Pit Bull owners. I have taken the liberty to publish part of the letter, plus an excerpt from a leaflet that accompanied the letter. I was very impressed with the accomplishments of these Schutzhund dogs, and upon reading the characteristics desired of the dog considered for training, I thought they had been written to describe the Pit Bull Terrier to a "T". The letter reads:

"I was recently made aware of your publication when I acquired two Pit Bull Terrier pups from Mr. John B. Reid. Both are line-bred from Dibo-strain stock, and are hard as nails. Mr. Reid and I hope to establish a name for these dogs in the sport of *Schutzhund* (protection dog) which is now a competitive sport in America. While I have been working dogs in and out of the military for some ten years, I had never tried a Pit until two and a half years ago, when I acquired a white Pit Bull from Oklahoma. This dog's hard body and aggressive attitude provided a challenge. Everything needed was there, but it was not easy to gain the necessary control for training, especially around other dogs.

This dog was named "Thunder", and he has certainly lived up to his name. During his training, he has firmly attached himself to a number of Shepherds and one Akita (with me firmly attached to him). More times than I care to remember, I was convinced that he could just not make it. Then he would hit the agitator's sleeve with more force and power than I ever dreamed possible and I would start all over again.

Well, to make a long story short, "Thunder" and I made it. We received our Schutzhund "A" title under Fred Pfeifle, a licensed Schutzhund judge, at the sanctioned match of the North American Working Dog Association. For those who have not encountered Schutzhund work before, I am enclosing a brief description of the work necessary for a Schutzhund title.

Any dog 18 inches at the shoulders or taller that can meet the rigorous requirements is eligible for competition. In my opinion, there are no dogs that can handle the work like a Pit Bull if the owner can handle the challenge.

Yours truly,
Caleb S. Douglas, President
American Obedience Dog Club"

A portion of the enclosed leaflet is as follows:

Schutzhund training is not for every trainer, nor for every dog. It is for the few dedicated sportsmen who want to take their dogs beyond the usual obedience routine. Those who want to bring forth the TRUE working capabilities of their breeds and who, by eliminating from the breeding program those dogs incapable of the required rigorous work, try to maintain the true character of our great working breeds.

What is a Schutzhund? He is not an attack dog, not a guard dog, not merely a protection dog. The Schutzhund is a dog who has earned a valid Schutzhund Degree in an official Schutzhund trial. He is a superbly-trained, versatile, all-around member of the family. He will perform equally well in the Obedience ring, on the track, in search and rescue, and in protecting defensively his owner, family, and home. He is trained to use considerable force to stop an assailant, and to quit when the assailant stops struggling. He will not attack on his own volition unless he or his master are directly threatened. He stops his "attack", which is in reality a defense, automatically when combat stops or when commanded to do so by his handler. He is the genuinely accepted family dog.

The tests that the Schutzhund must pass are quite rigorous. For instance, the dog must follow his owner's track, aged at least half an hour, for at least 440 yards, with at least two turns and two objects to be retrieved. The obedience portion of the trial consists of on-leash and off-leash heeling with gun shots being fired during the off-lead heeling; the usual stands, down, sits, some of them performed with the handler never stopping his movement; a sendaway of at least 75 feet; the recall; retrieving over a 40 inch hurdle, and a long down with the handler approximately 150 feet away from the dog with his back turned to the dog. This long down lasts through the entire obedience exam of the next dog, including the firing of the gun shots. The man-work (protection work) consists of quartering from blind to blind, finding the decoy, barking at the decoy but not touching him. At the command of the handler, the dog will go heel. The dog is led away while the decoy goes into a different hiding place. After the decoy is in his hiding place, handler and dog walk at heel, off-lead, towards the hiding place. At about 20 feet distance, the decoy will jump out of hiding and try to

310

attack the handler. The dog must go into action immediately without hesitation, keeping the attacker off his owner/handler. Following this test there is a courage test in which the dog is sent after his fleeing attacker. Just before the dog reaches him, the decoy turns and tries to drive the dog off the field. This action takes place approximately 150 feet away from the handler. The dog is completely on his own, and now he must display the native courage to move in and stop the attacker by seizing the protected arm.

Since the origin of Schutzhund training is in Europe, let us quickly examine the history and results of this training for dogs in Europe. At the turn of the century, the forerunner of the German Working Dog Association set the standard for police and working dogs, paying particular attention to the dog's character and his service to man. Its fundamentals are: temperament, courage, protection drive, fighting drive, toughness, sharpness, responsiveness, absence of fear, flight reflex, eagerness to please.

In this context, temperament is just one ingredient of character. The Schutzhund trial tests all the ingredients of character mentioned. NASA, the North American Working Dog Association is a non-profit organization, standardizing Schutzhund training and sanctioning trials. As a sport, NASA, as of this writing, divorce themselves completely from any commercialism, abhorring the incomplete and unfair "training" of the so-called "guard dog" or even the idiotic idea of the attack dog! It is the DOG and the SPORT that counts.

PIT BULLS ARE WHERE YOU FIND THEM.

Fred Nemiroff

(*Pit Bull Gazette,* February 1979)

Here in New York, the Alaskan Malamute club of Staten Island, the Siberian Husky club of Staten Island, as well as the Malamute club of Long Island, all hold weight-pulling contests during the winter. A good friend of mine has a team of Malamutes that have grown up with my Pit Bull "Scarlet". They played as pups and because they got along so well, my friend suggested that we try running "Scarlet" in the team. That is how I got started in the sport.

The first thing I had to do was get her used to a harness. I raised her as my house dog so she was used to walking on a lead. (I mean pulling on a lead.) All I did was start walking her with the harness instead of her collar. Next, I had to get her used to pulling weight behind her. I hooked her up to an old car tire and away she went. She needed very little encouragement. An old car tire is the best way to start a dog because it is dead weight, and if the dog stops pulling, the tire won't catch up to the dog and hit him from the rear and startle him. Next, I filled a kiddie cart (little red wagon) up with any weight I could find. I used three bowling balls, a portable T.V., a tool box full of tools, and lead chunks from work. I weighed everything I used, and it came to a total of 265 lbs. with the wagon. This looked like a good starting test. With everything loaded into my car, off to the park I went to try "Scarlet" out. When I got there, I unloaded the cart, the weight, the harness, and everything else I thought that I might need, and was ready to start. Unfortunately, I had forgotten one main necessity. My dog. I loaded everything back up, and went home to get "Scarlet". When I got back to the park the second time, I had everything I needed, including my faithful Pit Bull. My dog was finally hooked up and raring to go. The little red wagon was loaded to the hilt. My friend held "Scarlet" while I walked about 15 to 20 yards away. I screamed for my dog to come, and my friend let her go. At first she couldn't move it, so by instinct, she backed up and ran forward with all her speed. When she got to the end of the lead, it was like hitting a brick wall. She was thrown back and landed right on top of the wagon. It looked like she was watching the portable T.V. that I was using for weight. So her spirit wouldn't be broken, I removed one bowling ball and hooked her up again. I called her and this time she got it rolling. When she reached me, I rewarded her with a piece of meat (I knew she'd like it because I was pretty hungry and had tried a piece while she wasn't looking.) After two more good pulls, "Scarlet" knew what it was all about. I added the bowling ball, which I had removed and figured I'd end the day with this last pull. When the dog was ready, I called her. This time she knew how to lean into the weight and the wagon started to move. Little by little she was gaining speed and when she was ¾ of the way to me, I couldn't believe what happened! The axles on the cart bent and the whole thing collapsed. I immediately ran to her to reward her so she would feel like she had finished the run.

That's when I discovered that I had eaten all of the reward. Well, at least she had my praise. With a new and better wagon, and a couple of weeks of this type of training, I figured it was time to hook "Scarlet" up with my friend's team.

Off to a favorite trail where we hooked "Scarlet" up with three Malamutes. Two experienced dogs in the front, then "Scarlet" and last, another experienced dog. We wanted dogs in front of her, hoping that when they started running, she would run after them. (With the training I gave her with the red wagon, I knew she wouldn't worry about the weight behind her.) We had the last dog behind her so she wouldn't be right next to the cart, and be spooked by the noise. My friend drove the cart and I ran in front so "Scarlet" could see me. The brake was released and they were off. She was unbelievable. When I couldn't run any more, the team passed me and "Scarlet" continued on with the team. She couldn't care less if I was there or not. She was having a ball and was determined to catch the two dogs in front of her. When the team returned, I rewarded "Scarlet". (This time I used dog biscuits instead of meat figuring I wouldn't eat the biscuits. But I was wrong. When no one was looking, I tried one. That's when I discovered that I was cured. I didn't eat another dog biscuit all day.)

"Scarlet" ran with the team for about a month when my friend informed me of a Malamute club that was putting on a pulling contest. She was entering her strongest Malamute and talked me into entering "Scarlet". I knew nothing about the rules or anything until we went to the site and everything was explained to me. This is how the weight pulling contest was run.

If your dog has never pulled in a contest before, it costs $1.00 to qualify. If your dog qualifies, it costs another dollar to enter the contest. In order to qualify, your dog must pull the empty cart 15 yards from a standing start. The empty cart is made of steel and weighs 95 lbs. There are four weight classes:

Lightweight—up to 60 lbs.
Middleweight—61 to 85 lbs.
Heavyweight—86 to 125 lbs.
Super Heavyweights—125 lbs. and over
After the qualifying runs the contest begins. The first run was at

140 lbs. If the dog pulls it the fifteen yards in 90 seconds or less, he qualifies for the next round when more weight is added. If a dog fails at a certain weight, that weight is recorded along with the time it took him to pull the heaviest load he did pull. This is done in case two dogs fail at the same weight; the dog who pulled the last load fastest is the winner. If your dog fails at a given weight and another dog succeeds at that weight, your dog is eliminated from the contest. Your dog competes only against dogs in his weight class. The runway is between two fences with the front wheel of the cart sitting on the starting line. When the front wheel touches the finish line your dog has succeeded. A weight pulling harness is used (supplied by the club or you can use your own). This type of harness has a separator at the back which is behind the dog's back legs and tail. As the weight is increased, this type harness won't push down on the dog's back and restrict his pulling power.

The owner of the dog must stand behind the finish line at all times, but can bait his dog with food, calling, or anything he wishes but a bitch in heat. (Remember that this is a fun meet and the rules are a lot stricter at official contests). No dogs are allowed behind the starting line while a dog is pulling.

Well, enough with the rules. This is how it went with "Scarlet" in her first contest. She was 11 months old and was 41 lbs. This put her in the lightweight class against 3 Siberian Huskies and 1 Samoyed. (She qualified with ease).

140 lbs: "Scarlet" and all others succeeded.

180 lbs: Two Siberians were eliminated. "Scarlet" pulled good but 1 Siberian male (52 lbs) pulled the weight faster.

220 lbs: Samoyed eliminated. Siberian pulled good but struggled to get load started. Same thing with "Scarlet". (Siberian still faster).

260 lbs: Siberian couldn't move load and sat on line for 90 seconds. For 45 seconds, Scarlet couldn't get load moving but she never stopped trying and finally got the thing going. The contest is on grass and dirt and the wheels have a tendency to dig a rut as more weight is put on the cart. I kept encouraging her knowing

that if she kept it going she would make it to the finish. (I was so hyped up that I started chewing on the bait). "Scarlet" made it to the end and won 1st prize in the lightweight division.

She was the smallest dog there and everyone was so glad that she made it that they applauded her.

As she got older, I entered her in many more contests. She matured to 45 lbs and her best pull was 485 lbs. She was just too small to pull any more weight. To show you a comparison, the winning super heavyweight won with a pull of 725 lbs. There is no doubt in my mind that a big, sound, Pit Bull could equal or exceed that weight.

As time went on I started seeing a change in Scarlet's temperament. She started getting into trouble with the rest of the sled team so I thought it best to retire her from racing and just enter her in weight pulls.

"Scarlet" was my first Pit Bull. She was bred by Mr. Al Stebor of Middlesex, N.J. She is bred out of Red Devil/Corvino on the top and Clouse/Hemphill on the bottom.

I've had a lot of fun with "Scarlet" at the weight pulls and it is definitely another useful way to exercise and enjoy a Pit Bull.

I have taken the trouble to include these articles in order to demonstrate the versatility of the breed. This may seem at cross purposes to my other writings, as readers may recall that I earlier went to great pains to make the point that there was no such thing as an all-purpose dog. I still stand by that. However, as one reader wrote: "There may not be such a thing as an all purpose dog, but the American Pit Bull Terrier sure comes close to it!" Well, I agree, but we will enjoy our dogs more if we keep in mind their limitations and not allow ourselves to be blinded by our unrestrained admiration for the capabilities of the breed. While it is true that Pit Bulls have been trained to herd sheep, point birds and so on, we must be aware that the specialists in those areas will generally outshine our breed and there are some areas for which the breed is simply not suited. Take for instance guide dogs for the blind. There is just no way that our dogs are going to excel in this area. Oh, sure they will do well in training. In fact, as I recall, there was a sort of aptitude test for guide dogs that is given young pups and the single most important indicator was whether or not a pup would retrieve a ball. Now of all the Pit Bull pups I have raised, I can't recall any that didn't automatically retrieve a ball thrown for them. (I can remember smiling wryly and stating that they were good guide dog candidates.) So what is the fatal drawback? Simply that when a Pit Bull sees another dog, in his "delicious delirium" he will forget about his guide dog duties and his poor blind master will be in for a wild ride!

It is simply a case of one behavior overriding another. Clarence Pfaffenberger in his great little book *The New Knowledge of Dog Behavior* tells of retrievers being trained for sniffing out mines during World War II. Retrievers, because of their tractability and excellent noses, would have been my choice, too, for this type of work. However, at least some turned out not to be suitable. When live gunfire was sprayed over dogs and people crawling through a planted mine field to simulate combat conditions, a sea gull was hit and downed. The fall of the fluttering bird was too much for an Irish Water Spaniel. He jerked free of his handler, ran pell mell through the mine field and fetched his prize proudly back. If the mines had been live, of course, the dog and several people could have been killed. Such an overpowering urge to retrieve feathered prey would not interfere with a guide dog, however, because it would be a very uncommon thing for a bird to fall in the path of any typical person. Dogs, however, are not rare and that makes the majority of Pit Bulls unsuitable as guide dogs.

However, no Retriever, or any other breed for that matter, could do some of the amazing things of which the Pit Bull is capable. So we have no apology to make for our breed! It is unique and it commands respect—no matter how grudgingly given.

The breed is worth owning and worth defending. No po-

Champion Fred T, a conqueror of champions and a producer of champions.

tential owner should be discouraged from taking up the breed by anything I have said in this book. I have told about my misadventures in the legal system to demonstrate the folly of foolish felonies and the unreasonable stance taken by the animal welfare lunatics. The only reason I became a target for them was because I was highly visible as an author of numerous pieces that defended the breed and told the truth about dogfighting. Despite the proliferation of the foolish felonies, the stranglehold of the loonies on the legislators is weakening and support for the breed is growing stronger. More and more reputable and distinguished people are getting into raising Bulldogs. Even people of other breeds have rallied to the support of our breed. The good old Bulldog is not only invincible, he has proven irresistible. Indomitable under the worst of circumstances, he can but prosper in newer and more enlightened times.

APPENDIX A

Recommended Reading

Since owners of the American Pit Bull Terrier are popularly portrayed as ignorant in dog matters specifically and everything else in general, it behooves us all to become veritable amateur cynologists. Actually, it is fun to study and learn about our breed—no devotee has trouble with that—but it is also interesting and enjoyable to learn about dogs in general and other breeds in particular. (It helps us appreciate our own all the more!) The following books will start the reader on the road to becoming, if not a cynologist, at least a bona fide expert on dogs. However, as useful as book learning is, we must always keep in mind that some of the top experts on dogs never wrote a book. So don't close your mind completely to new knowledge simply because it is contradicted somewhere in print. For the reader's convenience, I am providing my own evaluation of each entry.

Books

Armitage, George C. *Thirty Years with Fighting Dogs.* Privately published, Washington, D.C. 1936.

This book has become a classic of sorts, even among show dog breeders, for it gives a stark look into the pit dog world of the thirties, at least Armitage's part of it. Armitage tells about many of the famous dogs of his day, gives accounts of matches, and he spends a good part of his book castigating his enemies. Advice on conditioning and nutrition are badly outdated.

Ash, Edward C. *Dogs: Their History and Development.* (Two volumes) Houghton Mifflin, Boston and New York, 1926.

Although published long ago, this is a classic work that is valuable reading for the serious student of dogs.

Colby, Joseph L. *The American Pit Bull Terrier.* Privately published, Sacramento, 1936.

Written by one of John P. Colby's sons, this little book contains many old photographs of dogs from the Colby line and gives accounts of matches of several dogs. It contains articles by other dog men, too—including an article on the breed by the founder of the United Kennel Club.

Davis, Henry P. editor. *The New Dog Encyclopedia.* Galahad Books, New York, 1970.

The best reasonably priced dog encyclopedia available, it gives information on the American Kennel Club show breeds and their show standards, but, unlike other so-called "complete" dog books, it does not pretend that there are no other breeds outside that body's, recognition. In fact, it gives information on such things as tree hounds and border collies. It also gives a history of the United Kennel Club and the American Field registry. It also has sections on field trials of various types (i.e. pointing dogs, retrievers, hounds, water races, and herding dog trials), sections on diseases and parasites, and information on training.

Denlinger, Milo G. *The Complete Pit Bull or Staffordshire Terrier.* Denlingers, Washington, D.C., 1948.

This book consists of a compilation of articles derived

319

from old *Bloodlines* magazines, from old books on the Staffordshire Bull Terrier, and from works on the American Staffordshire Terrier, as well as other sources. It can be confusing to beginners, but it contains many old photographs, articles on matches, expecially the old classic ones, and it contains historically significant old woodcuts and paintings. Despite all its faults, it was a quality book, excellently bound with good paper and high-quality photógraphs. It is now a collector's item, and the last price list I saw carried it at two hundred dollars a copy!

Eberhard, Ernest. *The New Complete Bull Terrier* Howell Book House Inc., New York, 1971.

A typical breed book, but of good quality, for those who want to learn about a breed that is often confused with ours.

Fox, Richard K. *The Dog Pit.* Police Gazette Publishers, New York, circa 1910.

This book was written by the editor of the *Police Gazette* magazine. To view this book in perspective, it is important for the reader to know that the *Police Gazette* was a combination *National Enquirer-Playboy-Sports Illustrated* of its times. Actually, I can't think of a comparable publication now. It covered many illegal sports of that time including boxing, wrestling, cockfighting, and dog fighting. So this book should by no means be considered an authoritative breed book, for it is full of much hogwash. The stories about fights between Bulldogs and bobcats and monkeys, etc., are probably all fabrications. It is an interesting book, though, and it contains drawings of such famous old dogs as Cincinnati Paddy and Crib. It also contains the *Police Gazette* rules for a pit contest.

Glass, Eugene. *The Sporting Bull Terrier.* Privately published, Battle Creek, 1910.

Mr. Glass was the editor of a pit dog magazine of that time called *The Dog Fancier.* It contains rules, a keep, instructions for building a kennel, and information on the use of training devices. What is amazing is the tremendous amount of misinformation that is contained in the book. Two examples will suffice: For the springpole, it is suggested that a coonskin be used as the part for the dog to grasp and hang from. Now any dog man who has ever tried a coonhide for this purpose knows that it very quickly disintegrates. The author also talks about the white show Bull Terrier as though it were just a fancy show version of the Pit Bulldog and "just as game." Ridiculous on both counts!

Little, Dr. Clarence C. *Inheritance of Coat Color in Dogs.* Comstock Publishing Company of Cornell University Press, Ithaca, N.Y., 1957

The classic work in this area.

Maffie, Frederic. *The Life of Humbug.* Manor Books, Inc., New York, 1979.

This is a fiction book, but it is written by a knowledgable dog man and contains much information on pit dogs.

Meeks, Jack. *Memoirs of the Pit.* Privately published by Pete Sparks. Starke, Florida, 1974

Although this book was published in 1974, the manuscript was actually compiled in the mid-thirties, so it is of interest historically.

Onscott, Kyle. *The New Art of Breeding Better Dogs.* Howell Book House, Inc., New York, 1973.

A very thorough treatise on the subject. It puts the bugaboos of inbreeding to rest.

Sequan Kim, a daughter of Going Light Jim and a granddaughter of the great dog, Mason's Hog.

322

The Freemans with three young dogs (left to right), Maggie, Angel, and Paddy, all Dibo dogs.

Pffaffenberger, Clarence. *The New Knowledge of Dog Behavior*. Howell Book House, Inc., New York, 1963.

This easy-to-read book gives out fairly technical knowledge on dogs in a very palatible manner. It dispels much nonsense about dog behavior and inbreeding. It deals with the training of dogs for various tasks, but primarily for the training (and selective breeding) of guide dogs for the blind.

Pierce, Rev. Thomas. *The Dog*. Cassel and Co. London, 1892.

Pierce wrote under the name of "Idestone," as it was the style of the day to use *nom de plumes,* and he perpetrated many wild tales about dog activities. There is no way to check them now, of course, and no one bothered to check them during his era. He was a controversial and promotion-minded figure of his times. Any would-be cynologist should be familiar with these types of writings, for they influenced those who came later.

Pollard, Jack, editor. *Wild Dogs, Working Dogs, Pedigreed, and Pets*. Lansdowne Press Limited, Melbourne, 1968.

This book is a compilation of numerous writings that appeared in magazines and newspapers in Australia and New Zealand clear back to the last century. Much of the writing concerns herding dogs and hunting dogs, but there is one section on fighting dogs, "Dogfight in Botany Bay", in which the reporter pooh-poohs the idea of cruelty in dogfighting, as "fighting is the breath of life to them". In addition to some very fine writings, the book is a treasure trove of historic pictures, but unfortunately not of Bulldogs.

Scott, John Paul and John L. Fuller. *The Genetic Basis of Dog Behavior*. University of Chicago Press, Chicago and London, 1965.

Youatt, William and E.J. Lewis. *The Dog*. Levitt and Allen, New York, 1846.

This is an American edition of a book that was originally published in London by Youatt in 1845. Any editions of this work are rare and hard to find, so the reader may have to resort to a library search and obtain it on either Xerox copies or microfilm.

Young, Stanley Paul. *The Wolf in North American History*. Caxton Printers, Caldwell, Idaho, 1946.

No one of his time knew wolves and coyotes better than Young.

Young, Stanley Paul. *The Clever Coyote*. Caxton Printers, Caldwell, Idaho. 1946.

Periodicals

American Field Weekly. American Field Publishing Co., 222 West Adams Street, Chicago, Ill. Mainly concerned with bird dogs and spaniels, but, again, we learn about our breed by studying others—especially the performance breeds. The Field Dog Stud Book is a highly-respected registry, and many field men utilize this registry only, in order to stay away from the A.K.C. show stock.

Animal Behavior. Bailliere Tendall, 7 & 8 Henrietta St., Covent Garden, London WC2E—8QE. This is a highly respected journal with technical articles on behavior of all animal species. For the serious cynologist.

Bloodlines Coonhound Journal. United Kennel Club, 321 West Cedar Street, Kalamazoo, Michigan. The coonhounds are the bulwark of the U.K.C. now, with many field trials

Gehres' Scaramouche.

Opposite:
Jim Isaacs and his show champion Sorrell's Crazy Snuffy.

and conformation shows being much larger than the A.K.C. dog shows—or field trials.

Bloodlines Journal. United Kennel Club, 321 West Cedar Street, Kalamazoo, Michigan. This magazine carries a section on the American Pit Bull Terrier in the back (they used to be featured in the front!), but the U.K.C. is very touchy about being connected with dog fighting. Consequently, many APBT fanciers are embittered about the extreme stance taken by the United Kennel Club (e.g. *Bloodlines* will not take advertisements for treadmills while *Dog World* does!). Ironically, if the humane-oriented groups ever thought they had disposed of dog fighting, the hound people would most likely be their next target!

Dog World. Judy-Berner Publishing Co., 469 Ohio Street., Chicago, Ill. Mainly concerned with show dogs, it occasionally published articles on show breeds with histories (dating back to the pharoahs!) that smack more of a lively imagination than scientific research. It generally contains some articles of general interest.

The Field. The Field, 8 Stratton Street, London W1, England. Articles on dogs and English field trials including those of herding dogs.

Full Cry. Walker Publishing Co., Inc., Box 190, Sedalia, Missouri. Contains stories about coon hunts and field trials. Some of the advertisements of equipment could be of conceivable use to Bulldog people.

Pit Bull Gazette. American Dog Breeders Association, Box 1771, Salt Lake City, Utah. Contains articles on all aspects of the American Pit Bull Terrier, and advertisements feature all the needs of the APBT devotee, including breaking sticks, treadmills, and harnesses. Featuring many fine articles, this magazine is pretty much the "flagship" of the breed now.

Pit Dog Report. P.O. Box 33509, Houston, Texas. This magazine is the oldest currently of the journals that report the results of pit contests. A subscriber has to have the recommendation of another pit dog man in order to receive the magazine.

Pit-Pal Magazine. P.O. Box 21201, Houston, Texas. Like the preceding journal, this one gives the results of matches, and it, too, requires a benefactor in order to subscribe. The title is reminiscent of *Pit and Pal,* a magazine that was put out by Bob Hemphill and others during the late thirties and early forties.

Sporting Dog Journal. P.O. Box 476, Jefferson, Georgia. Although not the oldest, this has been a very steady publication, always coming out just like clockwork. While intended for the pit dog man, non-sponsored inquiries will be considered (but not necessarily accepted).

APPENDIX B

Modern Pit Rules

Actually, the rules reproduced here were written by Al Brown countless years ago, and have been in my possession for many years. Mr. Brown is nearly a hundred years old now and still alive at this writing. His rules were a definite improvement over the United Kennel Club rules, and unlike U.K.C. rules, they are still used today. Modern dog men often use what they call "Cajun rules", but they are basically

Carlene Freeman with Dolly (registered as Betsy), a daughter of Going Light Barney.

Gehres' Danyo, a son of Dillinger and a grandson of Going Light Barney.

331

Al Brown rules with slight alterations. For example, instead of rule number 12A in which a dog has three seconds to leave his corner, he is usually given ten seconds to cross to the other dog. Also, a 30 second out-of-hold count is generally used, and the down dog must always scratch first (unless both dogs are down with neither in a position of advantage).

Finally, the pit may be covered with carpeting rather than canvas (rule number 3), the scratch lines may consist of some of the modern tapes, and the central line between the scratch lines is often omitted.

PIT RULES

Used For Contests Deciding
The Gamer of Two Dogs

(Game—Plucky, Unyielding in Manner, Ready and Willing)

By Al Brown

Rule 1:

The principals shall select a referee who is familiar with the rules and who is satisfactory to both sides. The referee will then appoint his timekeeper. Each handler will select a man to act as his chief second or cornerman, whose duties are to wash the opponent's dog, and to remain near this dog's corner as an observer.

Rule 2:

Each handler is to furnish two clean towels and a suitable blanket, to be used by his opponent. Either handler may demand that the opposing handler and his cornerman bare their arms to the elbows; also the handler may taste his opponent's dog's water before or after the contest (up until the referee has rendered his decision on the contest.)

Rule 3:

No water, sponges, towels or any other accessories are allowed in the pit at any time, except the referee who shall have in his possession an adequate breaking stick and a pencil, also a copy of these rules. The pit shall not be less than 14 feet each way, whenever possible, with sides 30 inches high, with a canvas covered floor, upon which has been painted or chalked on, 12 ½ feet apart, and with a center-line half way between the scratch-lines.

Rule 4:

The referee shall toss a coin to be called by the handlers. The winner of the toss shall decide which dog shall be washed first and also have the choice of corners.

Rule 5:

The dogs shall be washed at pit-side, in warm water and some approved washing powders and then rinsed. The first dog to be washed shall be brought in and held in the tub by his handler, and washed by the opposing cornerman. When pronounced clean by the referee, the dog shall be rinsed clean in a separate tub of warm water and toweled dry as possible, then wrapped in the blanket provided and carried to his appointed corner by his handler and accompanied by the man who washed him. These are the only two persons allowed near this dog until the dogs are LET GO. The other dog shall now be brought in and held in the tub by his handler and washed (in the same water) by the opposing corner-man. When this dog is pronounced clean by the referee and rinsed clean and toweled dry, he shall then be carried to his corner by his handler and accompanied by the man who washed him.

Rule 6:

The referee shall now ask "Are both corners ready?" If so, "Cornerman, out of the pit" . . . "Face your dogs" . . . "Let Go". The timekeeper shall note the time and write it down for future reference.

Rule 7:

Any dog who jumps the pit is automatically the loser of the contest and no scratches are necessary, and no dog is required or allowed to scratch to a dead dog. The live dog is the winner.

Opposite:
Greenwood's Clem. Sire: Tudor's Ace. Dam: Sonoma Cindy.

Fonseca's Brandy (age 1 year). Sire: Heinzl's Blind Ben. Dam: Fonseca's Goldy.

Rule 8:

Should either dog become fanged, the referee shall instruct the handlers to take hold of their dogs and try to hold them still so the handler can try to unfang his dog. If this isn't possible, the referee shall separate the dogs with the proper breaking stick and then unfang the dog, using a pencil. The referee will then order the handlers to set their dogs down near the center of the pit and approximately two feet apart. The referee will then order "Let Go". This in no way constitutes a turn or a handle and has no bearing on the future scratches.

Rule 9:

This is to be a fair Scratch-in-turn contest until the dogs quit fighting, then Rule 13 shall take over. The first dog to turn must scratch first; thereafter they are to scratch alternately (regardless of which dog turns) until one dog fails to scratch and thereby loses the contest.

Rule 10:

To be a fair turn, the dog accused of turning must turn his head and shoulders and his front feet away from the opponent and regardless of whether or not the dogs are otherwise touching.

Rule 11:

The referee shall call all turns, although either handler may ask for a turn on either dog. If the referee rules there has been a turn, he will instruct the handlers to "PICK UP FREE OF HOLDS" as soon as possible, and should either dog accidently get a hold again, the handlers shall set the dogs down immediately and make a continued effort to pick up the dogs, free of holds. When picked up, the dogs must be taken to their respective corners and faced away from their opponent. The timekeeper shall note the time and take up the count (not out loud) and also the referee shall notify the handler whose dog must scratch.

Rule 12:

At 25 seconds, the timekeeper shall call out "GET READY". At these instructions each handler must toe his scratch-line and face his dog toward his opponent with his dog's head and

336

shoulders showing fair from between his handler's legs, and the dog's four feet on the canvas floor. At the 30 seconds, the timekeeper calls out "LET GO", and the handler whose dog must scratch must instantly take his hands away from all contact with his dog and also release all leg pressure from against his dog's body. And the dog must instantly start across and the handler must remain behind his scratch-line until his dog has completed his scratch or the referee has ruled upon it. There is no time limit on the time required to complete this scratch. But, when released at the words "LET GO", the dog must start across to his opponent. He may waver from direct line, fall down, crawl . . . drag or push himself across, so long as he makes a continued effort and DOES NOT HESITATE OR STOP until he has reached and touched his opponent. The opposing handler may release his dog anytime he sees fit after the order to "LET GO"; however, he must do so as soon as the dogs have touched each other.

Rule 12A:

This is an alternate rule for those handlers who desire to have their dogs counted out in the corner. It is the same in all respects as Rule 12, except that after 30 seconds, when the timekeeper calls out "LET GO", the referee shall count out loud, at as near one-second intervals as possible, ONE . . . TWO . . . TIME (three seconds), and the dog must be out of his corner and on his way before the referee calls "TIME", or lose.

Rule 13

If the dogs have aparently quit fighting, whether they are helpless, tired out or curred out, and regardless of whether both dogs are down or one dog is down and the other dog is standing over him, but neither dog has a hold, the referee shall ask if they are willing to scratch-it-out, to a win or not. If so, they shall proceed to do so, but if either handler is unwilling, then the referee shall instruct the timekeeper to note the time and call time in two minutes. If either dog breaks time, then nothing has changed, but if, at the end of the two minutes, the dogs are in the same relative positions and neither dog has a hold, the referee shall order the handlers to handle (PICK UP FREE OF HOLDS) their dogs. When picked up, the dogs shall be taken to their corners and the

Rose's Red Cole, a show champion and well-bred dog.

Opposite above:
Gehres' Gus.

Opposite:
Sorrell's Crazy Morgan.

corner procedure is the same as in a normally called turn and handle. If there have been no previous turns or handles to establish the order of scratching, the dog who has been the longest without a hold (usually the down dog) to be scratched first, then, as soon as free of holds, the dogs shall be picked up and the other dog scratched. Should one dog fail or refuse his scratch, then the dog who failed shall lose the contest. If both dogs fail to scratch, the referee shall call it a no-contest, but should both dogs make their initial scratches, the handlers by mutual agreement may ask the referee for a draw decision. The referee will then rule it a draw. Otherwise, the contest shall continue, but in this manner: any time the dogs are not in holds and not fighting, the referee shall order the dogs to be handled and scratched alternately until one dog fails to scratch and thereby loses. No attention is paid to turns (after Rule 13 is invoked) except as a possible chance to handle. THE REFEREE HAS FULL AUTHORITY AND HIS DECISION IS FINAL IN ALL MATTERS.

Rule 14:
Fouls that will be just cause for losing a contest:
   A. To leave the pit, with or without the dog before the referee has ruled.
   B. To receive anything from outside the pit, or allow anyone outside the pit to touch or assist the dog.
   C. To push, drum, throw or spank, or in any way assist a dog across his scratch-line, except by encouraging him by voice.
   D. To step across the scratch-line before the dog has completed his scratch or the referee has ruled on it.
   E. To stomp on the pit floor or kick the pit sides, yell at or give orders to the opponent's dog, or (in the referee's opinion) do anything to distract or interfere with either dog while scratching or fighting to affect the outcome of the contest.
   F. To interfere with the opposing handler or touch either dog until the referee gives an order to handle the dogs.
   G. To use a "RUB", "POISON", or "HYPO" on either dog.

Rule 15:
   If there should be any outside interference before the contest has been concluded, the referee has full authority to call it a "NO

CONTEST" and shall name the time and place the contest is to be resumed and fought out to a referee's decision. (The same referee shall preside). Also, the referee shall insist that the dogs be washed and weighed (in the referee's presence), and the dogs shall weigh at the weights specified in the original articles of agreement, and to do this as many times as necessary to conclude the contest.

I believe both Rules 12 and 13 are important, but I believe Rule 13 is the most important rule ever written and it will do more good to curtail "DRAG FIGHTS" where one or both good dogs could be lost. This rule will invariably decide the proper winner and much quicker.

Lots of short or improperly bred dogs will make one or several scratches in good style when not too exhausted, but pick him up right away and continue to ask him to go back across, and you may be surprised at how quickly one you were proud of will stand in his corner. Only a DEEP GAME dog will contine to go back in and these dogs only should be used as breeding stock.

Sarona Hemphill Rocky.

Apache Mojo. Sire: Wise's Max, Jr. Dam: Weaver's Swamp Red Dotty.

ILLUSTRATIONS INDEX

"PR" Apache Gypsy. Sire: "PR" Wise's Max, Jr. Dam: "PR" Weaver's Swamp Red Dotty.

Apache Red Lady. Sire: Sinister Chopper. Dam: Weaver's Swamp Red Dotty.

INDEX